C-3847 CAREER EXAMINATION SERIES

This is your
PASSBOOK for...

Office Applications Specialist

Test Preparation Study Guide
Questions & Answers

COPYRIGHT NOTICE

This book is SOLELY intended for, is sold ONLY to, and its use is RESTRICTED to individual, bona fide applicants or candidates who qualify by virtue of having seriously filed applications for appropriate license, certificate, professional and/or promotional advancement, higher school matriculation, scholarship, or other legitimate requirements of education and/or governmental authorities.

This book is NOT intended for use, class instruction, tutoring, training, duplication, copying, reprinting, excerption, or adaptation, etc., by:

1) Other publishers
2) Proprietors and/or Instructors of "Coaching" and/or Preparatory Courses
3) Personnel and/or Training Divisions of commercial, industrial, and governmental organizations
4) Schools, colleges, or universities and/or their departments and staffs, including teachers and other personnel
5) Testing Agencies or Bureaus
6) Study groups which seek by the purchase of a single volume to copy and/or duplicate and/or adapt this material for use by the group as a whole without having purchased individual volumes for each of the members of the group
7) Et al.

Such persons would be in violation of appropriate Federal and State statutes.

PROVISION OF LICENSING AGREEMENTS – Recognized educational, commercial, industrial, and governmental institutions and organizations, and others legitimately engaged in educational pursuits, including training, testing, and measurement activities, may address request for a licensing agreement to the copyright owners, who will determine whether, and under what conditions, including fees and charges, the materials in this book may be used them. In other words, a licensing facility exists for the legitimate use of the material in this book on other than an individual basis. However, it is asseverated and affirmed here that the material in this book CANNOT be used without the receipt of the express permission of such a licensing agreement from the Publishers. Inquiries re licensing should be addressed to the company, attention rights and permissions department.

All rights reserved, including the right of reproduction in whole or in part, in any form or by any means, electronic or mechanical, including photocopying, recording, or by any information storage and retrieval system, without permission in writing from the Publisher.

Copyright © 2024 by
National Learning Corporation

212 Michael Drive, Syosset, NY 11791
(516) 921-8888 • www.passbooks.com
E-mail: info@passbooks.com

PASSBOOK® SERIES

THE *PASSBOOK® SERIES* has been created to prepare applicants and candidates for the ultimate academic battlefield – the examination room.

At some time in our lives, each and every one of us may be required to take an examination – for validation, matriculation, admission, qualification, registration, certification, or licensure.

Based on the assumption that every applicant or candidate has met the basic formal educational standards, has taken the required number of courses, and read the necessary texts, the *PASSBOOK® SERIES* furnishes the one special preparation which may assure passing with confidence, instead of failing with insecurity. Examination questions – together with answers – are furnished as the basic vehicle for study so that the mysteries of the examination and its compounding difficulties may be eliminated or diminished by a sure method.

This book is meant to help you pass your examination provided that you qualify and are serious in your objective.

The entire field is reviewed through the huge store of content information which is succinctly presented through a provocative and challenging approach – the question-and-answer method.

A climate of success is established by furnishing the correct answers at the end of each test.

You soon learn to recognize types of questions, forms of questions, and patterns of questioning. You may even begin to anticipate expected outcomes.

You perceive that many questions are repeated or adapted so that you can gain acute insights, which may enable you to score many sure points.

You learn how to confront new questions, or types of questions, and to attack them confidently and work out the correct answers.

You note objectives and emphases, and recognize pitfalls and dangers, so that you may make positive educational adjustments.

Moreover, you are kept fully informed in relation to new concepts, methods, practices, and directions in the field.

You discover that you are actually taking the examination all the time: you are preparing for the examination by "taking" an examination, not by reading extraneous and/or supererogatory textbooks.

In short, this PASSBOOK®, used directedly, should be an important factor in helping you to pass your test.

OFFICE APPLICATIONS SPECIALIST

DUTIES:
An employee in this class works and functions as a specialist in the utilization of a variety of office application software including word processing, statistical applications, database programs, spreadsheets for data maintenance and presentation, report generation software, presentation applications including software for graphics and desk-top publishing. The employee may provide training in the use of the software and systems. A position in the class will require the employee to work with administrators throughout the jurisdiction on specific projects, and the employee will be expected to develop required knowledges specific to the functions of the department or jurisdiction. Work is reviewed based upon output and effectiveness of applications developed. Does related work as required.

SCOPE OF THE EXAMINATION:
The written test will cover knowledge, skills, and/or abilities in such areas as:
1. Use and operation of PC's and related peripheral equipment;
2. Preparing written material;
3. Principles of providing user support;
4. Training users of computers.

HOW TO TAKE A TEST

I. YOU MUST PASS AN EXAMINATION

A. WHAT EVERY CANDIDATE SHOULD KNOW

Examination applicants often ask us for help in preparing for the written test. What can I study in advance? What kinds of questions will be asked? How will the test be given? How will the papers be graded?

As an applicant for a civil service examination, you may be wondering about some of these things. Our purpose here is to suggest effective methods of advance study and to describe civil service examinations.

Your chances for success on this examination can be increased if you know how to prepare. Those "pre-examination jitters" can be reduced if you know what to expect. You can even experience an adventure in good citizenship if you know why civil service exams are given.

B. WHY ARE CIVIL SERVICE EXAMINATIONS GIVEN?

Civil service examinations are important to you in two ways. As a citizen, you want public jobs filled by employees who know how to do their work. As a job seeker, you want a fair chance to compete for that job on an equal footing with other candidates. The best-known means of accomplishing this two-fold goal is the competitive examination.

Exams are widely publicized throughout the nation. They may be administered for jobs in federal, state, city, municipal, town or village governments or agencies.

Any citizen may apply, with some limitations, such as the age or residence of applicants. Your experience and education may be reviewed to see whether you meet the requirements for the particular examination. When these requirements exist, they are reasonable and applied consistently to all applicants. Thus, a competitive examination may cause you some uneasiness now, but it is your privilege and safeguard.

C. HOW ARE CIVIL SERVICE EXAMS DEVELOPED?

Examinations are carefully written by trained technicians who are specialists in the field known as "psychological measurement," in consultation with recognized authorities in the field of work that the test will cover. These experts recommend the subject matter areas or skills to be tested; only those knowledges or skills important to your success on the job are included. The most reliable books and source materials available are used as references. Together, the experts and technicians judge the difficulty level of the questions.

Test technicians know how to phrase questions so that the problem is clearly stated. Their ethics do not permit "trick" or "catch" questions. Questions may have been tried out on sample groups, or subjected to statistical analysis, to determine their usefulness.

Written tests are often used in combination with performance tests, ratings of training and experience, and oral interviews. All of these measures combine to form the best-known means of finding the right person for the right job.

II. HOW TO PASS THE WRITTEN TEST

A. NATURE OF THE EXAMINATION

To prepare intelligently for civil service examinations, you should know how they differ from school examinations you have taken. In school you were assigned certain definite pages to read or subjects to cover. The examination questions were quite detailed and usually emphasized memory. Civil service exams, on the other hand, try to discover your present ability to perform the duties of a position, plus your potentiality to learn these duties. In other words, a civil service exam attempts to predict how successful you will be. Questions cover such a broad area that they cannot be as minute and detailed as school exam questions.

In the public service similar kinds of work, or positions, are grouped together in one "class." This process is known as *position-classification*. All the positions in a class are paid according to the salary range for that class. One class title covers all of these positions, and they are all tested by the same examination.

B. FOUR BASIC STEPS

1) Study the announcement

How, then, can you know what subjects to study? Our best answer is: "Learn as much as possible about the class of positions for which you've applied." The exam will test the knowledge, skills and abilities needed to do the work.

Your most valuable source of information about the position you want is the official exam announcement. This announcement lists the training and experience qualifications. Check these standards and apply only if you come reasonably close to meeting them.

The brief description of the position in the examination announcement offers some clues to the subjects which will be tested. Think about the job itself. Review the duties in your mind. Can you perform them, or are there some in which you are rusty? Fill in the blank spots in your preparation.

Many jurisdictions preview the written test in the exam announcement by including a section called "Knowledge and Abilities Required," "Scope of the Examination," or some similar heading. Here you will find out specifically what fields will be tested.

2) Review your own background

Once you learn in general what the position is all about, and what you need to know to do the work, ask yourself which subjects you already know fairly well and which need improvement. You may wonder whether to concentrate on improving your strong areas or on building some background in your fields of weakness. When the announcement has specified "some knowledge" or "considerable knowledge," or has used adjectives like "beginning principles of..." or "advanced ... methods," you can get a clue as to the number and difficulty of questions to be asked in any given field. More questions, and hence broader coverage, would be included for those subjects which are more important in the work. Now weigh your strengths and weaknesses against the job requirements and prepare accordingly.

3) Determine the level of the position

Another way to tell how intensively you should prepare is to understand the level of the job for which you are applying. Is it the entering level? In other words, is this the position in which beginners in a field of work are hired? Or is it an intermediate or advanced level? Sometimes this is indicated by such words as "Junior" or "Senior" in the class title. Other jurisdictions use Roman numerals to designate the level – Clerk I, Clerk II, for example. The word "Supervisor" sometimes appears in the title. If the level is not indicated by the title, check the description of duties. Will you be working under very close supervision, or will you have responsibility for independent decisions in this work?

4) Choose appropriate study materials

Now that you know the subjects to be examined and the relative amount of each subject to be covered, you can choose suitable study materials. For beginning level jobs, or even advanced ones, if you have a pronounced weakness in some aspect of your training, read a modern, standard textbook in that field. Be sure it is up to date and has general coverage. Such books are normally available at your library, and the librarian will be glad to help you locate one. For entry-level positions, questions of appropriate difficulty are chosen – neither highly advanced questions, nor those too simple. Such questions require careful thought but not advanced training.

If the position for which you are applying is technical or advanced, you will read more advanced, specialized material. If you are already familiar with the basic principles of your field, elementary textbooks would waste your time. Concentrate on advanced textbooks and technical periodicals. Think through the concepts and review difficult problems in your field.

These are all general sources. You can get more ideas on your own initiative, following these leads. For example, training manuals and publications of the government agency which employs workers in your field can be useful, particularly for technical and professional positions. A letter or visit to the government department involved may result in more specific study suggestions, and certainly will provide you with a more definite idea of the exact nature of the position you are seeking.

III. KINDS OF TESTS

Tests are used for purposes other than measuring knowledge and ability to perform specified duties. For some positions, it is equally important to test ability to make adjustments to new situations or to profit from training. In others, basic mental abilities not dependent on information are essential. Questions which test these things may not appear as pertinent to the duties of the position as those which test for knowledge and information. Yet they are often highly important parts of a fair examination. For very general questions, it is almost impossible to help you direct your study efforts. What we can do is to point out some of the more common of these general abilities needed in public service positions and describe some typical questions.

1) General information

Broad, general information has been found useful for predicting job success in some kinds of work. This is tested in a variety of ways, from vocabulary lists to questions about current events. Basic background in some field of work, such as sociology or economics, may be sampled in a group of questions. Often these are principles which have become familiar to most persons through exposure rather than through formal training. It is difficult to advise you how to study for these questions; being alert to the world around you is our best suggestion.

2) Verbal ability

An example of an ability needed in many positions is verbal or language ability. Verbal ability is, in brief, the ability to use and understand words. Vocabulary and grammar tests are typical measures of this ability. Reading comprehension or paragraph interpretation questions are common in many kinds of civil service tests. You are given a paragraph of written material and asked to find its central meaning.

3) Numerical ability

Number skills can be tested by the familiar arithmetic problem, by checking paired lists of numbers to see which are alike and which are different, or by interpreting charts and graphs. In the latter test, a graph may be printed in the test booklet which you are asked to use as the basis for answering questions.

4) Observation

A popular test for law-enforcement positions is the observation test. A picture is shown to you for several minutes, then taken away. Questions about the picture test your ability to observe both details and larger elements.

5) Following directions

In many positions in the public service, the employee must be able to carry out written instructions dependably and accurately. You may be given a chart with several columns, each column listing a variety of information. The questions require you to carry out directions involving the information given in the chart.

6) Skills and aptitudes

Performance tests effectively measure some manual skills and aptitudes. When the skill is one in which you are trained, such as typing or shorthand, you can practice. These tests are often very much like those given in business school or high school courses. For many of the other skills and aptitudes, however, no short-time preparation can be made. Skills and abilities natural to you or that you have developed throughout your lifetime are being tested.

Many of the general questions just described provide all the data needed to answer the questions and ask you to use your reasoning ability to find the answers. Your best preparation for these tests, as well as for tests of facts and ideas, is to be at your physical and mental best. You, no doubt, have your own methods of getting into an exam-taking mood and keeping "in shape." The next section lists some ideas on this subject.

IV. KINDS OF QUESTIONS

Only rarely is the "essay" question, which you answer in narrative form, used in civil service tests. Civil service tests are usually of the short-answer type. Full instructions for answering these questions will be given to you at the examination. But in case this is your first experience with short-answer questions and separate answer sheets, here is what you need to know:

1) Multiple-choice Questions

Most popular of the short-answer questions is the "multiple choice" or "best answer" question. It can be used, for example, to test for factual knowledge, ability to solve problems or judgment in meeting situations found at work.

A multiple-choice question is normally one of three types—
- It can begin with an incomplete statement followed by several possible endings. You are to find the one ending which *best* completes the statement, although some of the others may not be entirely wrong.
- It can also be a complete statement in the form of a question which is answered by choosing one of the statements listed.

- It can be in the form of a problem – again you select the best answer.

Here is an example of a multiple-choice question with a discussion which should give you some clues as to the method for choosing the right answer:

When an employee has a complaint about his assignment, the action which will *best* help him overcome his difficulty is to
    A. discuss his difficulty with his coworkers
    B. take the problem to the head of the organization
    C. take the problem to the person who gave him the assignment
    D. say nothing to anyone about his complaint

In answering this question, you should study each of the choices to find which is best. Consider choice "A" – Certainly an employee may discuss his complaint with fellow employees, but no change or improvement can result, and the complaint remains unresolved. Choice "B" is a poor choice since the head of the organization probably does not know what assignment you have been given, and taking your problem to him is known as "going over the head" of the supervisor. The supervisor, or person who made the assignment, is the person who can clarify it or correct any injustice. Choice "C" is, therefore, correct. To say nothing, as in choice "D," is unwise. Supervisors have and interest in knowing the problems employees are facing, and the employee is seeking a solution to his problem.

2) True/False Questions

The "true/false" or "right/wrong" form of question is sometimes used. Here a complete statement is given. Your job is to decide whether the statement is right or wrong.

SAMPLE: A roaming cell-phone call to a nearby city costs less than a non-roaming call to a distant city.

This statement is wrong, or false, since roaming calls are more expensive.
This is not a complete list of all possible question forms, although most of the others are variations of these common types. You will always get complete directions for answering questions. Be sure you understand *how* to mark your answers – ask questions until you do.

V. RECORDING YOUR ANSWERS

Computer terminals are used more and more today for many different kinds of exams.
For an examination with very few applicants, you may be told to record your answers in the test booklet itself. Separate answer sheets are much more common. If this separate answer sheet is to be scored by machine – and this is often the case – it is highly important that you mark your answers correctly in order to get credit.
An electronic scoring machine is often used in civil service offices because of the speed with which papers can be scored. Machine-scored answer sheets must be marked with a pencil, which will be given to you. This pencil has a high graphite content which responds to the electronic scoring machine. As a matter of fact, stray dots may register as answers, so do not let your pencil rest on the answer sheet while you are pondering the correct answer. Also, if your pencil lead breaks or is otherwise defective, ask for another.

Since the answer sheet will be dropped in a slot in the scoring machine, be careful not to bend the corners or get the paper crumpled.

The answer sheet normally has five vertical columns of numbers, with 30 numbers to a column. These numbers correspond to the question numbers in your test booklet. After each number, going across the page are four or five pairs of dotted lines. These short dotted lines have small letters or numbers above them. The first two pairs may also have a "T" or "F" above the letters. This indicates that the first two pairs only are to be used if the questions are of the true-false type. If the questions are multiple choice, disregard the "T" and "F" and pay attention only to the small letters or numbers.

Answer your questions in the manner of the sample that follows:

32. The largest city in the United States is
    A. Washington, D.C.
    B. New York City
    C. Chicago
    D. Detroit
    E. San Francisco

1) Choose the answer you think is best. (New York City is the largest, so "B" is correct.)
2) Find the row of dotted lines numbered the same as the question you are answering. (Find row number 32)
3) Find the pair of dotted lines corresponding to the answer. (Find the pair of lines under the mark "B.")
4) Make a solid black mark between the dotted lines.

VI. BEFORE THE TEST

Common sense will help you find procedures to follow to get ready for an examination. Too many of us, however, overlook these sensible measures. Indeed, nervousness and fatigue have been found to be the most serious reasons why applicants fail to do their best on civil service tests. Here is a list of reminders:

- Begin your preparation early – Don't wait until the last minute to go scurrying around for books and materials or to find out what the position is all about.
- Prepare continuously – An hour a night for a week is better than an all-night cram session. This has been definitely established. What is more, a night a week for a month will return better dividends than crowding your study into a shorter period of time.
- Locate the place of the exam – You have been sent a notice telling you when and where to report for the examination. If the location is in a different town or otherwise unfamiliar to you, it would be well to inquire the best route and learn something about the building.
- Relax the night before the test – Allow your mind to rest. Do not study at all that night. Plan some mild recreation or diversion; then go to bed early and get a good night's sleep.
- Get up early enough to make a leisurely trip to the place for the test – This way unforeseen events, traffic snarls, unfamiliar buildings, etc. will not upset you.
- Dress comfortably – A written test is not a fashion show. You will be known by number and not by name, so wear something comfortable.

- Leave excess paraphernalia at home – Shopping bags and odd bundles will get in your way. You need bring only the items mentioned in the official notice you received; usually everything you need is provided. Do not bring reference books to the exam. They will only confuse those last minutes and be taken away from you when in the test room.
- Arrive somewhat ahead of time – If because of transportation schedules you must get there very early, bring a newspaper or magazine to take your mind off yourself while waiting.
- Locate the examination room – When you have found the proper room, you will be directed to the seat or part of the room where you will sit. Sometimes you are given a sheet of instructions to read while you are waiting. Do not fill out any forms until you are told to do so; just read them and be prepared.
- Relax and prepare to listen to the instructions
- If you have any physical problem that may keep you from doing your best, be sure to tell the test administrator. If you are sick or in poor health, you really cannot do your best on the exam. You can come back and take the test some other time.

VII. AT THE TEST

The day of the test is here and you have the test booklet in your hand. The temptation to get going is very strong. Caution! There is more to success than knowing the right answers. You must know how to identify your papers and understand variations in the type of short-answer question used in this particular examination. Follow these suggestions for maximum results from your efforts:

1) Cooperate with the monitor
The test administrator has a duty to create a situation in which you can be as much at ease as possible. He will give instructions, tell you when to begin, check to see that you are marking your answer sheet correctly, and so on. He is not there to guard you, although he will see that your competitors do not take unfair advantage. He wants to help you do your best.

2) Listen to all instructions
Don't jump the gun! Wait until you understand all directions. In most civil service tests you get more time than you need to answer the questions. So don't be in a hurry. Read each word of instructions until you clearly understand the meaning. Study the examples, listen to all announcements and follow directions. Ask questions if you do not understand what to do.

3) Identify your papers
Civil service exams are usually identified by number only. You will be assigned a number; you must not put your name on your test papers. Be sure to copy your number correctly. Since more than one exam may be given, copy your exact examination title.

4) Plan your time
Unless you are told that a test is a "speed" or "rate of work" test, speed itself is usually not important. Time enough to answer all the questions will be provided, but this does not mean that you have all day. An overall time limit has been set. Divide the total time (in minutes) by the number of questions to determine the approximate time you have for each question.

5) Do not linger over difficult questions

If you come across a difficult question, mark it with a paper clip (useful to have along) and come back to it when you have been through the booklet. One caution if you do this – be sure to skip a number on your answer sheet as well. Check often to be sure that you have not lost your place and that you are marking in the row numbered the same as the question you are answering.

6) Read the questions

Be sure you know what the question asks! Many capable people are unsuccessful because they failed to *read* the questions correctly.

7) Answer all questions

Unless you have been instructed that a penalty will be deducted for incorrect answers, it is better to guess than to omit a question.

8) Speed tests

It is often better NOT to guess on speed tests. It has been found that on timed tests people are tempted to spend the last few seconds before time is called in marking answers at random – without even reading them – in the hope of picking up a few extra points. To discourage this practice, the instructions may warn you that your score will be "corrected" for guessing. That is, a penalty will be applied. The incorrect answers will be deducted from the correct ones, or some other penalty formula will be used.

9) Review your answers

If you finish before time is called, go back to the questions you guessed or omitted to give them further thought. Review other answers if you have time.

10) Return your test materials

If you are ready to leave before others have finished or time is called, take ALL your materials to the monitor and leave quietly. Never take any test material with you. The monitor can discover whose papers are not complete, and taking a test booklet may be grounds for disqualification.

VIII. EXAMINATION TECHNIQUES

1) Read the general instructions carefully. These are usually printed on the first page of the exam booklet. As a rule, these instructions refer to the timing of the examination; the fact that you should not start work until the signal and must stop work at a signal, etc. If there are any *special* instructions, such as a choice of questions to be answered, make sure that you note this instruction carefully.

2) When you are ready to start work on the examination, that is as soon as the signal has been given, read the instructions to each question booklet, underline any key words or phrases, such as *least, best, outline, describe* and the like. In this way you will tend to answer as requested rather than discover on reviewing your paper that you *listed without describing*, that you selected the *worst* choice rather than the *best* choice, etc.

3) If the examination is of the objective or multiple-choice type – that is, each question will also give a series of possible answers: A, B, C or D, and you are called upon to select the best answer and write the letter next to that answer on your answer paper – it is advisable to start answering each question in turn. There may be anywhere from 50 to 100 such questions in the three or four hours allotted and you can see how much time would be taken if you read through all the questions before beginning to answer any. Furthermore, if you come across a question or group of questions which you know would be difficult to answer, it would undoubtedly affect your handling of all the other questions.

4) If the examination is of the essay type and contains but a few questions, it is a moot point as to whether you should read all the questions before starting to answer any one. Of course, if you are given a choice – say five out of seven and the like – then it is essential to read all the questions so you can eliminate the two that are most difficult. If, however, you are asked to answer all the questions, there may be danger in trying to answer the easiest one first because you may find that you will spend too much time on it. The best technique is to answer the first question, then proceed to the second, etc.

5) Time your answers. Before the exam begins, write down the time it started, then add the time allowed for the examination and write down the time it must be completed, then divide the time available somewhat as follows:
    - If 3-1/2 hours are allowed, that would be 210 minutes. If you have 80 objective-type questions, that would be an average of 2-1/2 minutes per question. Allow yourself no more than 2 minutes per question, or a total of 160 minutes, which will permit about 50 minutes to review.
    - If for the time allotment of 210 minutes there are 7 essay questions to answer, that would average about 30 minutes a question. Give yourself only 25 minutes per question so that you have about 35 minutes to review.

6) The most important instruction is to *read each question* and make sure you know what is wanted. The second most important instruction is to *time yourself properly* so that you answer every question. The third most important instruction is to *answer every question*. Guess if you have to but include something for each question. Remember that you will receive no credit for a blank and will probably receive some credit if you write something in answer to an essay question. If you guess a letter – say "B" for a multiple-choice question – you may have guessed right. If you leave a blank as an answer to a multiple-choice question, the examiners may respect your feelings but it will not add a point to your score. Some exams may penalize you for wrong answers, so in such cases *only*, you may not want to guess unless you have some basis for your answer.

7) Suggestions
    a. Objective-type questions
        1. Examine the question booklet for proper sequence of pages and questions
        2. Read all instructions carefully
        3. Skip any question which seems too difficult; return to it after all other questions have been answered
        4. Apportion your time properly; do not spend too much time on any single question or group of questions

5. Note and underline key words – *all, most, fewest, least, best, worst, same, opposite*, etc.
6. Pay particular attention to negatives
7. Note unusual option, e.g., unduly long, short, complex, different or similar in content to the body of the question
8. Observe the use of "hedging" words – *probably, may, most likely*, etc.
9. Make sure that your answer is put next to the same number as the question
10. Do not second-guess unless you have good reason to believe the second answer is definitely more correct
11. Cross out original answer if you decide another answer is more accurate; do not erase until you are ready to hand your paper in
12. Answer all questions; guess unless instructed otherwise
13. Leave time for review

   b. Essay questions
   1. Read each question carefully
   2. Determine exactly what is wanted. Underline key words or phrases.
   3. Decide on outline or paragraph answer
   4. Include many different points and elements unless asked to develop any one or two points or elements
   5. Show impartiality by giving pros and cons unless directed to select one side only
   6. Make and write down any assumptions you find necessary to answer the questions
   7. Watch your English, grammar, punctuation and choice of words
   8. Time your answers; don't crowd material

8) Answering the essay question

Most essay questions can be answered by framing the specific response around several key words or ideas. Here are a few such key words or ideas:

M's: manpower, materials, methods, money, management
P's: purpose, program, policy, plan, procedure, practice, problems, pitfalls, personnel, public relations
   a. Six basic steps in handling problems:
   1. Preliminary plan and background development
   2. Collect information, data and facts
   3. Analyze and interpret information, data and facts
   4. Analyze and develop solutions as well as make recommendations
   5. Prepare report and sell recommendations
   6. Install recommendations and follow up effectiveness

   b. Pitfalls to avoid
   1. *Taking things for granted* – A statement of the situation does not necessarily imply that each of the elements is necessarily true; for example, a complaint may be invalid and biased so that all that can be taken for granted is that a complaint has been registered

2. *Considering only one side of a situation* – Wherever possible, indicate several alternatives and then point out the reasons you selected the best one
3. *Failing to indicate follow up* – Whenever your answer indicates action on your part, make certain that you will take proper follow-up action to see how successful your recommendations, procedures or actions turn out to be
4. *Taking too long in answering any single question* – Remember to time your answers properly

IX. AFTER THE TEST

Scoring procedures differ in detail among civil service jurisdictions although the general principles are the same. Whether the papers are hand-scored or graded by machine we have described, they are nearly always graded by number. That is, the person who marks the paper knows only the number – never the name – of the applicant. Not until all the papers have been graded will they be matched with names. If other tests, such as training and experience or oral interview ratings have been given, scores will be combined. Different parts of the examination usually have different weights. For example, the written test might count 60 percent of the final grade, and a rating of training and experience 40 percent. In many jurisdictions, veterans will have a certain number of points added to their grades.

After the final grade has been determined, the names are placed in grade order and an eligible list is established. There are various methods for resolving ties between those who get the same final grade – probably the most common is to place first the name of the person whose application was received first. Job offers are made from the eligible list in the order the names appear on it. You will be notified of your grade and your rank as soon as all these computations have been made. This will be done as rapidly as possible.

People who are found to meet the requirements in the announcement are called "eligibles." Their names are put on a list of eligible candidates. An eligible's chances of getting a job depend on how high he stands on this list and how fast agencies are filling jobs from the list.

When a job is to be filled from a list of eligibles, the agency asks for the names of people on the list of eligibles for that job. When the civil service commission receives this request, it sends to the agency the names of the three people highest on this list. Or, if the job to be filled has specialized requirements, the office sends the agency the names of the top three persons who meet these requirements from the general list.

The appointing officer makes a choice from among the three people whose names were sent to him. If the selected person accepts the appointment, the names of the others are put back on the list to be considered for future openings.

That is the rule in hiring from all kinds of eligible lists, whether they are for typist, carpenter, chemist, or something else. For every vacancy, the appointing officer has his choice of any one of the top three eligibles on the list. This explains why the person whose name is on top of the list sometimes does not get an appointment when some of the persons lower on the list do. If the appointing officer chooses the second or third eligible, the No. 1 eligible does not get a job at once, but stays on the list until he is appointed or the list is terminated.

X. HOW TO PASS THE INTERVIEW TEST

The examination for which you applied requires an oral interview test. You have already taken the written test and you are now being called for the interview test – the final part of the formal examination.

You may think that it is not possible to prepare for an interview test and that there are no procedures to follow during an interview. Our purpose is to point out some things you can do in advance that will help you and some good rules to follow and pitfalls to avoid while you are being interviewed.

What is an interview supposed to test?

The written examination is designed to test the technical knowledge and competence of the candidate; the oral is designed to evaluate intangible qualities, not readily measured otherwise, and to establish a list showing the relative fitness of each candidate – as measured against his competitors – for the position sought. Scoring is not on the basis of "right" and "wrong," but on a sliding scale of values ranging from "not passable" to "outstanding." As a matter of fact, it is possible to achieve a relatively low score without a single "incorrect" answer because of evident weakness in the qualities being measured.

Occasionally, an examination may consist entirely of an oral test – either an individual or a group oral. In such cases, information is sought concerning the technical knowledges and abilities of the candidate, since there has been no written examination for this purpose. More commonly, however, an oral test is used to supplement a written examination.

Who conducts interviews?

The composition of oral boards varies among different jurisdictions. In nearly all, a representative of the personnel department serves as chairman. One of the members of the board may be a representative of the department in which the candidate would work. In some cases, "outside experts" are used, and, frequently, a businessman or some other representative of the general public is asked to serve. Labor and management or other special groups may be represented. The aim is to secure the services of experts in the appropriate field.

However the board is composed, it is a good idea (and not at all improper or unethical) to ascertain in advance of the interview who the members are and what groups they represent. When you are introduced to them, you will have some idea of their backgrounds and interests, and at least you will not stutter and stammer over their names.

What should be done before the interview?

While knowledge about the board members is useful and takes some of the surprise element out of the interview, there is other preparation which is more substantive. It *is* possible to prepare for an oral interview – in several ways:

1) Keep a copy of your application and review it carefully before the interview

This may be the only document before the oral board, and the starting point of the interview. Know what education and experience you have listed there, and the sequence and dates of all of it. Sometimes the board will ask you to review the highlights of your experience for them; you should not have to hem and haw doing it.

2) Study the class specification and the examination announcement

Usually, the oral board has one or both of these to guide them. The qualities, characteristics or knowledges required by the position sought are stated in these documents. They offer valuable clues as to the nature of the oral interview. For example, if the job involves supervisory responsibilities, the announcement will usually indicate that knowledge of modern supervisory methods and the qualifications of the candidate as a supervisor will be tested. If so, you can expect such questions, frequently in the form of a hypothetical situation which you are expected to solve. NEVER go into an oral without knowledge of the duties and responsibilities of the job you seek.

3) Think through each qualification required

Try to visualize the kind of questions you would ask if you were a board member. How well could you answer them? Try especially to appraise your own knowledge and background in each area, *measured against the job sought*, and identify any areas in which you are weak. Be critical and realistic – do not flatter yourself.

4) Do some general reading in areas in which you feel you may be weak

For example, if the job involves supervision and your past experience has NOT, some general reading in supervisory methods and practices, particularly in the field of human relations, might be useful. Do NOT study agency procedures or detailed manuals. The oral board will be testing your understanding and capacity, not your memory.

5) Get a good night's sleep and watch your general health and mental attitude

You will want a clear head at the interview. Take care of a cold or any other minor ailment, and of course, no hangovers.

What should be done on the day of the interview?

Now comes the day of the interview itself. Give yourself plenty of time to get there. Plan to arrive somewhat ahead of the scheduled time, particularly if your appointment is in the fore part of the day. If a previous candidate fails to appear, the board might be ready for you a bit early. By early afternoon an oral board is almost invariably behind schedule if there are many candidates, and you may have to wait. Take along a book or magazine to read, or your application to review, but leave any extraneous material in the waiting room when you go in for your interview. In any event, relax and compose yourself.

The matter of dress is important. The board is forming impressions about you – from your experience, your manners, your attitude, and your appearance. Give your personal appearance careful attention. Dress your best, but not your flashiest. Choose conservative, appropriate clothing, and be sure it is immaculate. This is a business interview, and your appearance should indicate that you regard it as such. Besides, being well groomed and properly dressed will help boost your confidence.

Sooner or later, someone will call your name and escort you into the interview room. *This is it.* From here on you are on your own. It is too late for any more preparation. But remember, you asked for this opportunity to prove your fitness, and you are here because your request was granted.

What happens when you go in?

The usual sequence of events will be as follows: The clerk (who is often the board stenographer) will introduce you to the chairman of the oral board, who will introduce you to the other members of the board. Acknowledge the introductions before you sit down. Do not be surprised if you find a microphone facing you or a stenotypist sitting by. Oral interviews are usually recorded in the event of an appeal or other review.

Usually the chairman of the board will open the interview by reviewing the highlights of your education and work experience from your application – primarily for the benefit of the other members of the board, as well as to get the material into the record. Do not interrupt or comment unless there is an error or significant misinterpretation; if that is the case, do not hesitate. But do not quibble about insignificant matters. Also, he will usually ask you some question about your education, experience or your present job – partly to get you to start talking and to establish the interviewing "rapport." He may start the actual questioning, or turn it over to one of the other members. Frequently, each member undertakes the questioning on a particular area, one in which he is perhaps most competent, so you can expect each member to participate in the examination. Because time is limited, you may also expect some rather abrupt switches in the direction the questioning takes, so do not be upset by it. Normally, a board member will not pursue a single line of questioning unless he discovers a particular strength or weakness.

After each member has participated, the chairman will usually ask whether any member has any further questions, then will ask you if you have anything you wish to add. Unless you are expecting this question, it may floor you. Worse, it may start you off on an extended, extemporaneous speech. The board is not usually seeking more information. The question is principally to offer you a last opportunity to present further qualifications or to indicate that you have nothing to add. So, if you feel that a significant qualification or characteristic has been overlooked, it is proper to point it out in a sentence or so. Do not compliment the board on the thoroughness of their examination -- they have been sketchy, and you know it. If you wish, merely say, "No thank you, I have nothing further to add." This is a point where you can "talk yourself out" of a good impression or fail to present an important bit of information. Remember, *you close the interview yourself.*

The chairman will then say, "That is all, Mr. _____, thank you." Do not be startled; the interview is over, and quicker than you think. Thank him, gather your belongings and take your leave. Save your sigh of relief for the other side of the door.

How to put your best foot forward

Throughout this entire process, you may feel that the board individually and collectively is trying to pierce your defenses, seek out your hidden weaknesses and embarrass and confuse you. Actually, this is not true. They are obliged to make an appraisal of your qualifications for the job you are seeking, and they want to see you in your best light. Remember, they must interview all candidates and a non-cooperative candidate may become a failure in spite of their best efforts to bring out his qualifications. Here are 15 suggestions that will help you:

1) Be natural – Keep your attitude confident, not cocky

If you are not confident that you can do the job, do not expect the board to be. Do not apologize for your weaknesses, try to bring out your strong points. The board is interested in a positive, not negative, presentation. Cockiness will antagonize any board member and make him wonder if you are covering up a weakness by a false show of strength.

2) Get comfortable, but don't lounge or sprawl

Sit erectly but not stiffly. A careless posture may lead the board to conclude that you are careless in other things, or at least that you are not impressed by the importance of the occasion. Either conclusion is natural, even if incorrect. Do not fuss with your clothing, a pencil or an ashtray. Your hands may occasionally be useful to emphasize a point; do not let them become a point of distraction.

3) Do not wisecrack or make small talk

This is a serious situation, and your attitude should show that you consider it as such. Further, the time of the board is limited – they do not want to waste it, and neither should you.

4) Do not exaggerate your experience or abilities

In the first place, from information in the application or other interviews and sources, the board may know more about you than you think. Secondly, you probably will not get away with it. An experienced board is rather adept at spotting such a situation, so do not take the chance.

5) If you know a board member, do not make a point of it, yet do not hide it

Certainly you are not fooling him, and probably not the other members of the board. Do not try to take advantage of your acquaintanceship – it will probably do you little good.

6) Do not dominate the interview

Let the board do that. They will give you the clues – do not assume that you have to do all the talking. Realize that the board has a number of questions to ask you, and do not try to take up all the interview time by showing off your extensive knowledge of the answer to the first one.

7) Be attentive

You only have 20 minutes or so, and you should keep your attention at its sharpest throughout. When a member is addressing a problem or question to you, give him your undivided attention. Address your reply principally to him, but do not exclude the other board members.

8) Do not interrupt

A board member may be stating a problem for you to analyze. He will ask you a question when the time comes. Let him state the problem, and wait for the question.

9) Make sure you understand the question

Do not try to answer until you are sure what the question is. If it is not clear, restate it in your own words or ask the board member to clarify it for you. However, do not haggle about minor elements.

10) Reply promptly but not hastily

A common entry on oral board rating sheets is "candidate responded readily," or "candidate hesitated in replies." Respond as promptly and quickly as you can, but do not jump to a hasty, ill-considered answer.

11) Do not be peremptory in your answers

A brief answer is proper – but do not fire your answer back. That is a losing game from your point of view. The board member can probably ask questions much faster than you can answer them.

12) Do not try to create the answer you think the board member wants

He is interested in what kind of mind you have and how it works – not in playing games. Furthermore, he can usually spot this practice and will actually grade you down on it.

13) Do not switch sides in your reply merely to agree with a board member

Frequently, a member will take a contrary position merely to draw you out and to see if you are willing and able to defend your point of view. Do not start a debate, yet do not surrender a good position. If a position is worth taking, it is worth defending.

14) Do not be afraid to admit an error in judgment if you are shown to be wrong

The board knows that you are forced to reply without any opportunity for careful consideration. Your answer may be demonstrably wrong. If so, admit it and get on with the interview.

15) Do not dwell at length on your present job

The opening question may relate to your present assignment. Answer the question but do not go into an extended discussion. You are being examined for a *new* job, not your present one. As a matter of fact, try to phrase ALL your answers in terms of the job for which you are being examined.

Basis of Rating

Probably you will forget most of these "do's" and "don'ts" when you walk into the oral interview room. Even remembering them all will not ensure you a passing grade. Perhaps you did not have the qualifications in the first place. But remembering them will help you to put your best foot forward, without treading on the toes of the board members.

Rumor and popular opinion to the contrary notwithstanding, an oral board wants you to make the best appearance possible. They know you are under pressure – but they also want to see how you respond to it as a guide to what your reaction would be under the pressures of the job you seek. They will be influenced by the degree of poise you display, the personal traits you show and the manner in which you respond.

ABOUT THIS BOOK

This book contains tests divided into Examination Sections. Go through each test, answering every question in the margin. We have also attached a sample answer sheet at the back of the book that can be removed and used. At the end of each test look at the answer key and check your answers. On the ones you got wrong, look at the right answer choice and learn. Do not fill in the answers first. Do not memorize the questions and answers, but understand the answer and principles involved. On your test, the questions will likely be different from the samples. Questions are changed and new ones added. If you understand these past questions you should have success with any changes that arise. Tests may consist of several types of questions. We have additional books on each subject should more study be advisable or necessary for you. Finally, the more you study, the better prepared you will be. This book is intended to be the last thing you study before you walk into the examination room. Prior study of relevant texts is also recommended. NLC publishes some of these in our Fundamental Series. Knowledge and good sense are important factors in passing your exam. Good luck also helps. So now study this Passbook, absorb the material contained within and take that knowledge into the examination. Then do your best to pass that exam.

EXAMINATION SECTION

EXAMINATION SECTION
TEST 1

DIRECTIONS: Each question or incomplete statement is followed by several suggested answers or completions. Select the one that BEST answers the question or completes the statement. *PRINT THE LETTER OF THE CORRECT ANSWER IN THE SPACE AT THE RIGHT.*

1. Which one of the following is considered a word processor program? 1.____
   A. Microsoft Word
   B. Microsoft Works
   C. Notepad
   D. Both A and B

2. Default headings are available under the _____ tab. 2.____
   A. Insert   B. Home   C. File   D. View

3. _____ deals with font, alignment and margins. 3.____
   A. Selecting   B. Formatting   C. Composing   D. Pattern

4. Which one of the following is the BEST format for storing bit-mapped images on the computer? 4.____
   A. .JPG   B. .PNG   C. .GIF   D. .TIF

5. A header specifies an area in the _____ margins of every page. 5.____
   A. top   B. bottom   C. left   D. right

6. When an Excel file is inserted into a Word document, the data is 6.____
   A. hyperlinked
   B. placed in a Word table
   C. linked
   D. embedded

7. A workbook in Excel is a file that 7.____
   A. is primarily used to generate graphs
   B. is often used for word processing
   C. can contain many sheets, chart sheets and worksheets
   D. both A and B

8. Excel can produce chart types that include 8.____
   A. only line graphs
   B. bar charts, line graphs and pie charts
   C. line graphs and pie charts only
   D. bar charts and line graphs only

9. In PowerPoint, the motion path is a 9.____
   A. method of moving items on the slide
   B. method of advancing slides
   C. indentation
   D. type of animation

10. _____ replaces similar words in a document.
    A. Word Count B. Thesaurus C. Wrap Text D. Format Printer

11. The MOST simple description of the Internet is
    A. a single network
    B. a huge collection of different networks
    C. collection of LANs
    D. single WAN

12. How can a computer be connected to the Internet?
    A. Through internet service providers B. Internet society
    C. Internet architecture board D. Local area network

13. A software program that is used to view web pages is known as a(n)
    A. Internet browser B. interpreter
    C. operating system D. website

14. Which of the following is used to search anything on the Internet?
    A. Search engines B. Routers
    C. Social networks D. Websites

15. When a website is accessed, its main page is called
    A. home page B. back end page
    C. dead end D. both A and B

16. Google Docs provides _____, which is a salient feature of Google Doc.
    A. image processing B. synchronization
    C. both A and B D. installation

17. Documents in Google Drive could be accessed from
    A. only a personal computer
    B. any computer that has Internet connection
    C. only that computer that has Google drive on hard disk
    D. both B and C

18. In an email address, for example test@gmail.com, "gmail" is known as
    A. domain
    B. host computer in commercial domain
    C. internet service provider
    D. URL

19. Which of the following is NOT a well-known domain?
    A. .edu B. .com C. .org D. .army

20. Cyberspace is an alternative name used for
    A. Internet B. information C. virtual space D. data space

21. Which one of the following is NOT an Internet browser?
    A. Chrome B. Firefly C. Firefox D. Safari

22. Which of the following is NOT a past or current search engine? 22.____
    A. Apple   B. Lycos   C. Bing   D. Google

23. Document scanning could be done through 23.____
    A. OCR   B. OMR
    C. both A and B   D. dot-matrix printer

24. _____ are used to fill out empty fields in scanned images of data. 24.____
    A. Computerized optical scanners   B. OCR software
    C. Scanners   D. Laser printers

25. All of the following are examples of hardware for standard home use EXCEPT 25.____
    A. flash drives   B. inkjet printers
    C. servers   D. laser printers

KEY (CORRECT ANSWERS)

1. D
2. B
3. B
4. D
5. A

6. B
7. C
8. B
9. A
10. B

11. B
12. A
13. A
14. A
15. A

16. B
17. B
18. B
19. D
20. A

21. B
22. A
23. C
24. A
25. C

TEST 2

DIRECTIONS: Each question or incomplete statement is followed by several suggested answers or completions. Select the one that BEST answers the question or completes the statement. *PRINT THE LETTER OF THE CORRECT ANSWER IN THE SPACE AT THE RIGHT.*

1. In a spreadsheet, data is organized in the form of
   - A. lines and spaces
   - B. rows and columns
   - C. layers and planes
   - D. height and width

2. Which one of the following menus is used to protect a worksheet?
   - A. Edit
   - B. Format
   - C. Data
   - D. Tools

3. _____ corrects spelling mistakes automatically.
   - A. Word wrap
   - B. AutoCorrect
   - C. Spell checker
   - D. Thesaurus

4. Which function is used to automatically align text?
   - A. Justification
   - B. Indentation
   - C. Both A and B
   - D. None of the above

5. Orientation is the property of the _____ function.
   - A. Print
   - B. Design
   - C. Image
   - D. Both A and B

6. Special effects that are used to present slides in a presentation are known as
   - A. effects
   - B. custom animation
   - C. transition
   - D. present animation

7. Page setup and print functions can typically be found in the _____ menu.
   - A. tools
   - B. format
   - C. file
   - D. edit

8. Which one of the following is considered removable storage media?
   - A. Scanner
   - B. Flash drive
   - C. External hard drive
   - D. Both B and C

9. Which component of the computer is called the brain of the computer?
   - A. ALU
   - B. Memory
   - C. Control Unit
   - D. CPU

10. .txt is a file that is named for _____ files.
    - A. Notepad
    - B. Word
    - C. Paint
    - D. Excel

11. Software programs that are automatically downloaded and work within a browser are known as
    - A. plug-in
    - B. utilities
    - C. widgets
    - D. add-on

12. _____ is a computer that requests data from other computers on the Internet.
    A. Client B. Server C. Super computer D. Personal computer

13. A wizard is considered as a _____ file with prompt display.
    A. system B. program C. help D. application

14. E-mails from unknown senders go into the _____ folder.
    A. Spam B. Trash C. Drafts D. Inbox

15. LAN is an abbreviation for _____ area network.
    A. line B. local C. large D. limited

16. Which of the following is NOT an extension for an image file?
    A. .bmp B. .jpg C. .png D. .xls

17. In the e-mail address *test@gmail.com*, "test" is the _____ name.
    A. domain B. user C. server D. ISP

18. To e-mail multiple recipients while hiding the recipients from view, use the ___ function.
    A. BCC B. CC C. send D. hide

19. The system that translates an IP address into a simple form that is easy to remember is
    A. domain name system B. domain
    C. domain numbering system D. server domain

20. Which one of the following is the CORRECT method to send a file through e-mail?
    A. CC B. Attachment
    C. Embed through HTML D. Both A and B

21. Inkjet printers are categorized as a(n) _____ printer.
    A. character B. ink C. line D. band

22. Which one of the following is a storage medium that has a shape of a circular plate?
    A. Disk B. CPU C. ALU D. Printer

23. Ctrl+P activates the _____ function.
    A. reboot B. save C. print D. paint

24. The file extension .exe represents an _____ file.
    A. examination B. extra C. executable D. extension

25. Which of the following is NOT considered an input device?
    A. OCR
    B. Optical scanner
    C. Printer
    D. Keyboard

25._____

KEY (CORRECT ANSWERS)

1. B
2. D
3. B
4. A
5. A

6. C
7. C
8. D
9. D
10. A

11. B
12. A
13. C
14. A
15. B

16. D
17. B
18. A
19. A
20. B

21. C
22. A
23. C
24. C
25. C

TEST 3

DIRECTIONS: Each question or incomplete statement is followed by several suggested answers or completions. Select the one that BEST answers the question or completes the statement. *PRINT THE LETTER OF THE CORRECT ANSWER IN THE SPACE AT THE RIGHT.*

1. Excel is a _____ program.
   A. graphics
   B. word processor
   C. spreadsheet
   D. typewriter

   1._____

2. Basically, a word processor program like Microsoft Word is a replacement for
   A. manual work
   B. typewriters
   C. both A and B
   D. graphical programs

   2._____

3. Which one of the following could be added as a sound effect to a PowerPoint presentation?
   A. .wav files and .mid files
   B. .wav files and .gif files
   C. .wav files and .jpg files
   D. .jpg files and .gif files

   3._____

4. Google Drive is an example of _____ software.
   A. system   B. application   C. database   D. firmware

   4._____

5. PDF stands for _____ document format.
   A. portable   B. picture   C. plain   D. private

   5._____

6. Which one of the following is an example of internal memory of a computer?
   A. Disks   B. Pen drive   C. RAM   D. CDs

   6._____

7. A keyboard is an example of a(n) _____ device.
   A. input
   B. output
   C. word processor
   D. printing

   7._____

8. Clip art is a collection of _____ that can be inserted into a document.
   A. text files
   B. image files
   C. templates
   D. audio files

   8._____

9. _____ is a distinctive part of memory which holds the contents temporarily during cut or copy functions.
   A. Clipboard   B. Macro   C. Template   D. Clip art

   9._____

10. _____ is a process to store files on a computer from the Internet.
    A. Uploading
    B. Downloading
    C. Pulling
    D. Transferring

    10._____

11. "Cut and paste" refers to
    A. deleting and moving text
    B. restoring and updating software
    C. cleaning images
    D. replacing images

    11._____

7

12. Which one of the following is a compressed format for images?
    A. GIF   B. JPGE   C. PNG   D. JPG

13. A computer stores information and data inside the
    A. hard drive   B. CPU   C. CD   D. monitor

14. WWW is an abbreviation of
    A. world wide web   B. wide world web
    C. web worldwide   D. world wide website

15. A _____ computer holds more than one processor.
    A. multithread   B. multi-unit
    C. multiprocessor   D. multiprogramming

16. Landscape and portrait are properties of
    A. page layout   B. design   C. formatting   D. text

17. _____ includes the company's name, address, phone number and e-mail address.
    A. Letterhead   B. Template   C. Visiting Card   D. Brochure

18. _____ Server provides database services for other computers.
    A. Application   B. Web   C. Database   D. FTP

19. Which one of the following is responsible for storing movies, images and pictures?
    A. File server   B. Web server
    C. Database server   D. Application server

20. GUI stands for graphical
    A. user interface   B. unified instrument
    C. unified interface   D. user instrument

21. Scanner is an example of a(n) _____ device.
    A. output   B. input   C. printing   D. both A and B

22. Which one of the following is NOT an example of computer hardware?
    A. Printer   B. Scanner   C. Mouse   D. Antivirus

23. Which one of the following provides the BEST quality reproduction of graphics?
    A. Laser printer   B. Inkjet printer
    C. Dot-matrix printer   D. Plotter

24. If an e-mail sender is unknown, then do not download the _____ because it might contain a virus.
    A. attachment   B. email
    C. spam   D. both A and B

25. The BEST way to send identical emails to more than one person is to   25.____
    A. use the CC option   B. add email ID to address
    C. forward   D. both A and B

KEY (CORRECT ANSWERS)

1.	C	11.	A
2.	B	12.	A
3.	A	13.	A
4.	B	14.	A
5.	A	15.	C
6.	C	16.	A
7.	A	17.	A
8.	B	18.	C
9.	A	19.	A
10.	B	20.	A

21.	B
22.	D
23.	D
24.	A
25.	A

TEST 4

DIRECTIONS: Each question or incomplete statement is followed by several suggested answers or completions. Select the one that BEST answers the question or completes the statement. *PRINT THE LETTER OF THE CORRECT ANSWER IN THE SPACE AT THE RIGHT.*

1. A keyboard shortcut for saving files is
   A. Alt+S   B. Ctrl+S   C. Ctrl+SV   D. S+Enter

   1.____

2. Which of the following is NOT a term relevant to Excel?
   A. slide
   B. cell
   C. formula
   D. column

   2.____

3. A _____ background is a grainy and non-smooth surface.
   A. texture   B. gradient   C. solid   D. pattern

   3.____

4. Word wrap forces all text to fit within the defined
   A. margin   B. indent   C. block   D. box

   4.____

5. In Microsoft Word, overview of the prepared document could be better seen through
   A. Preview
   B. Print Preview
   C. Review
   D. both A and B

   5.____

6. The amount of vertical space between text line in a document is known as
   A. double space
   B. line spacing
   C. single space
   D. vertical spacing

   6.____

7. Which one of the following devices is required for Internet connection?
   A. Joy stick   B. Modem   C. NIC card   D. Optical drive

   7.____

8. IBM is a short form used for
   A. Internal Business Management
   B. International Business Management
   C. Internal Business Machines
   D. International Business Machines

   8.____

9. Which one of the following is static and non-volatile memory?
   A. RAM   B. ROM   C. BIOS   D. Cache

   9.____

10. One disadvantage of Google Docs is
    A. less storage
    B. compatibility
    C. needs connectivity to Internet
    D. synchronization

    10.____

11. WAN is an abbreviation of _____ area network.
    A. wide   B. wired   C. whole   D. while

    11.____

12. Bibliography can be created through the _____ tab.
    A. References B. Design C. Review D. Insert

13. The _____ is MOST likely shared in a computer network.
    A. keyboard B. speaker C. printer D. scanner

14. A normal computer is not able to boot if it does not have a(n)
    A. operating system
    B. complier
    C. loader
    D. assembler

15. _____ is another name for junk e-mails.
    A. Spam B. Spoof C. Spool D. Sniffer scripts

16. A table of contents can be created automatically by using an option in
    A. Page Layout B. Insert C. References D. View

17. ALU stands for
    A. arithmetic logic unit
    B. array logic unit
    C. application logic unit
    D. both A and B

18. Orientation is concerned with the _____ set-up of the page.
    A. horizontal B. vertical C. both A and B D. spacing

19. _____ is a form of written communication within the same company which comprises guide words as heading.
    A. Memorandum
    B. Letterhead
    C. Template
    D. None of the above

20. Which one of the following is NOT a web browser?
    A. Chrome B. Opera C. Firefox D. Drupal

21. .net domain is specifically used for
    A. international organization
    B. internet infrastructure and service providers
    C. educational institutes
    D. commercial business

22. A modem is not required when the Internet is connected through
    A. Wi-Fi
    B. LAN
    C. dial-up phone
    D. cable

23. Mail Merge uses _____ to create separate copies of a document for multiple people in Microsoft Word.
    A. primary document
    B. data document
    C. both A and B
    D. web page

24. Linux is an example of
    A. operating system
    B. malware
    C. firmware
    D. application program

25. Which one of the following is a CORRECT format for a website address?   25._____
    A. www@com
    B. www.test.com
    C. www.test25A@com
    D. www#TeST.com

KEY (CORRECT ANSWERS)

1. B
2. A
3. B
4. A
5. B

6. B
7. B
8. D
9. B
10. C

11. A
12. A
13. C
14. A
15. A

16. C
17. A
18. C
19. A
20. D

21. B
22. A
23. C
24. A
25. B

EXAMINATION SECTION
TEST 1

DIRECTIONS: Each question or incomplete statement is followed by several suggested answers or completions. Select the one that BEST answers the question or completes the statement. *PRINT THE LETTER OF THE CORRECT ANSWER IN THE SPACE AT THE RIGHT.*

1. Physical components of computers are known as 1.____
   A. software   B. hardware   C. firmware   D. human ware

2. A touchscreen is considered a(n) _____ device. 2.____
   A. input   B. output   C. display   D. both A and B

3. Keyboards and microphones are examples of computer 3.____
   A. peripherals   B. software   C. add-ons   D. uploads

4. Unauthorized access to a computer is prevented through the use of 4.____
   A. passwords
   B. user logins
   C. access control software
   D. computer keys

5. In order to establish an Internet connection, a modem is always connected to a 5.____
   A. keyboard   B. monitor
   C. telephone line   D. printer

6. _____ does NOT hold data permanently. 6.____
   A. RAM   B. ROM   C. Hard drive   D. Flash drive

7. Identification of a user who comes back to the same website is done through the use of 7.____
   A. scripts   B. plug-in   C. cookies   D. both A and B

8. File _____ is the process of moving a file from one computer to another computer across the network. 8.____
   A. encryption   B. transfer   C. copying   D. updating

9. _____ is a type of software that controls specific hardware. 9.____
   A. Driver   B. Browser   C. Plug-in   D. Control panel

10. _____ is a downloadable program that is used for Internet surfing. 10.____
    A. Messenger   B. Firefox
    C. Windows Explorer   D. Internet

11. In Microsoft Word, _____ is NOT a font style. 11.____
    A. Bold   B. Regular   C. Superscript   D. Italic

13

12. Which of the following is NOT associated with page margins in a Word document?
    A. Top B. Center C. Left D. Right

13. Microsoft Office is a type of _____ software.
    A. application B. system C. Internet D. website

14. A function that is inside another function is known as a(n) _____ function.
    A. round B. nested C. sum D. average

15. To write a formula in Microsoft Excel, a user would start by typing
    A. % B. = C. # D. @

16. The individual boxes used for data entry in an Excel file are known as
    A. cells
    B. data points
    C. formulas
    D. squares

17. In PowerPoint, _____ do NOT show with the slide layout.
    A. titles B. animations C. lists D. charts

18. _____ is a basic option when looking for colorful images or graphics to publish in a PowerPoint presentation.
    A. Clip art
    B. Online search
    C. MS Paint
    D. Drawing

19. In a web browser, the addresses of Internet pages are known as
    A. web pages B. URLs C. scripts D. plug-in

20. A company that provides Internet services is called a(n)
    A. ISP B. IBM C. LAN D. Both A and B

21. _____ is the process of copying a file from personal computer to a remote computer.
    A. Downloading
    B. Uploading
    C. Updating
    D. Modification

22. _____ is a text that opens another page when clicked.
    A. Link
    B. Hyperlink
    C. Both A and B
    D. Web page

23. Dots per inch is the measure of printing
    A. quality B. type C. time D. layout

24. _____ is the collection of computers connected with each other.
    A. Group B. Team C. Network D. Meeting

25. Which one of the following is considered a high-end printer?
    A. Dot matrix printer
    B. Inkjet printer
    C. Laser
    D. Thermal

KEY (CORRECT ANSWERS)

1. B
2. D
3. A
4. A
5. C

6. A
7. C
8. B
9. A
10. B

11. C
12. B
13. A
14. B
15. B

16. A
17. B
18. A
19. B
20. A

21. B
22. C
23. A
24. C
25. C

TEST 2

DIRECTIONS: Each question or incomplete statement is followed by several suggested answers or completions. Select the one that BEST answers the question or completes the statement. *PRINT THE LETTER OF THE CORRECT ANSWER IN THE SPACE AT THE RIGHT.*

1. Which one of the following is a storage device?
   A. Printer
   B. Hard drive
   C. Scanner
   D. Motherboard

   1._____

2. DVD is an example of a(n) _____ disk.
   A. hard
   B. optical
   C. magnetic
   D. floppy

   2._____

3. _____ computers provide resources to other computers across the network.
   A. Server
   B. Client
   C. Framework
   D. Digital

   3._____

4. Random access memory is considered _____ computer memory.
   A. non-volatile
   B. volatile
   C. cache
   D. permanent

   4._____

5. Which one of the following is NOT an operating system?
   A. Windows
   B. IOS
   C. Android
   D. MS Office

   5._____

6. A(n) _____ is a person who gets illegal access to a computer system and steals information.
   A. administrator
   B. computer operator
   C. hacker
   D. programmer

   6._____

7. Which one of the following is NOT application software?
   A. MS Word
   B. Media player
   C. Linux
   D. MS Power Point

   7._____

8. Which one of the following represents a domain name?
   A. .com
   B. www
   C. URL
   D. HTTP

   8._____

9. _____ is NOT an example of an Internet browser.
   A. Opera
   B. Google
   C. Mozilla
   D. Internet Explorer

   9._____

10. Which one of the following is/was NOT a search engine?
    A. Altavista
    B. Bing
    C. Yahoo
    D. Facebook

    10._____

11. E-mail is an abbreviation of
    A. electronic mail
    B. easy mail
    C. electric email
    D. both A and B

    11._____

16

2 (#2)

12. A(n) _____ is a person who takes care of websites for large companies. 12._____
    A. administrator   B. webmaster
    C. programmer   D. hacker

13. _____ connect web pages with each other. 13._____
    A. Connecters   B. Links   C. Hyperlinks   D. Browsers

14. _____ is a program that is harmful for computers. 14._____
    A. Spam   B. Virus
    C. Operating system   D. Plug-in

15. CC is an abbreviation of _____ in emails. 15._____
    A. core copy   B. copycat
    C. carbon copy   D. copy copy

16. Software most commonly used for basic personal computing is 16._____
    A. Excel   B. SPSS   C. Illustrator   D. Dreamweaver

17. _____ is an option to send the same letter to different persons. 17._____
    A. Template   B. Macros   C. Mail Merge   D. Layout

18. Which one of the following is a file extension for MS Word? 18._____
    A. .doc   B. .txt   C. .bmp   D. .pdf

19. _____ displays the number of words in a document. 19._____
    A. Character Count   B. Word Count   C. Word Wrap   D. Thesaurus

20. In an Excel sheet, an active cell is specified with 20._____
    A. dotted border   B. dark wide border
    C. italic text   D. a dotted border

21. A(n) _____ is a file that contains rows and columns. 21._____
    A. database   B. spreadsheet
    C. word   D. drawing

22. _____ are objects on the slides that hold text in a PowerPoint presentation. 22._____
    A. Placeholders   B. Text holders
    C. Auto layouts   D. Object holders

23. Which one of the following brings up the first slide in a PowerPoint presentation? 23._____
    A. Ctrl+End   B. Ctrl+Home
    C. Page up   D. Next slide button

24. Which one of the following sends printing commands to a printer? 24._____
    A. F5   B. Ctrl+P   C. Ctrl+S   D. F12

25. Scanners are used to capture _____ copy of documents. 25._____
    A. soft   B. hard   C. single   D. first

KEY (CORRECT ANSWERS)

1. B
2. B
3. A
4. B
5. D

6. C
7. C
8. A
9. B
10. D

11. A
12. B
13. C
14. B
15. C

16. A
17. C
18. A
19. B
20. B

21. B
22. A
23. B
24. B
25. B

TEST 3

DIRECTIONS: Each question or incomplete statement is followed by several suggested answers or completions. Select the one that BEST answers the question or completes the statement. *PRINT THE LETTER OF THE CORRECT ANSWER IN THE SPACE AT THE RIGHT.*

1. Which one of the following is the MOST appropriate operation to move a text block in MS Word?
   A. Cut
   B. Save As
   C. Cut and Paste
   D. Copy and Paste

2. The Navigation pane opens under the _____ tab.
   A. View
   B. Review
   C. Page Layout
   D. Mailings

3. Ctrl+B makes selected test
   A. italic
   B. bold
   C. bigger
   D. uppercase

4. _____ is NOT an acceptable formula in Excel.
   A. 10+50
   B. =10+50
   C. =B7+B8
   D. =B7*B8

5. A worksheet usually contains _____ columns.
   A. 128
   B. 256
   C. 512
   D. 320

6. _____ is the process of getting data from the cell that is located in different worksheets.
   A. Accessing
   B. Referencing
   C. Updating
   D. Functioning

7. The shortcut _____ selects all PowerPoint slides at once.
   A. Ctrl+Home
   B. Ctrl+A
   C. Alt+Home
   D. Shift+A

8. By pressing Ctrl+V in a Word document, the user
   A. pastes text
   B. cuts and pastes text
   C. adds a video box
   D. deletes a page

9. Transitions are applicable only on
   A. Excel worksheets
   B. PowerPoint slides
   C. image files
   D. Word document

10. In MS Word, the _____ tab has options for margin, orientation and spacing.
    A. Design
    B. Review
    C. Page Layout
    D. Insert

11. Which one of the following is graphic software?
    A. MS Office
    B. Adobe Photoshop
    C. Firefox
    D. Notepad

12. Which one of the following is a social networking website?
    A. Facebook
    B. Yahoo
    C. Google
    D. ASK

13. A computer monitor is referred to as a(n) _____ device.
    A. output   B. input   C. sound   D. printing

14. _____ memory is another name for the main memory of the computer.
    A. Primary   B. Direct   C. Simple   D. Quick

15. An operating system is _____ software.
    A. application   B. system   C. editing   D. both A and C

16. Which one of the following pieces of equipment is necessary for video calls?
    A. Webcam   B. Mouse   C. Scanner   D. Printer

17. _____ is a primary input device that is used to enter text and numbers.
    A. Mouse   B. Keyboard   C. Joystick   D. Microphone

18. Of the following, which is NOT an example of a web browser?
    A. Firefox   B. Opera   C. Chrome   D. Google Talk

19. A _____ is a collection of many web pages that are related to each other.
    A. web browser   B. website
    C. search engine   D. Firefox

20. Which one of the following is considered a personal journal used for posts?
    A. Blog   B. E-mail   C. Chat   D. Messengers

21. Windows _____ provides security against external threats.
    A. antivirus   B. spyware   C. firmware   D. firewall

22. Desktop and laptop computers are different from each other in terms of _____ and cost.
    A. operating system   B. functions
    C. physical structure   D. application software

23. _____ is a process of stealing confidential information without permission of the user.
    A. Forwarding   B. Hacking   C. Searching   D. Complaining

24. RAM is located in the _____ board.
    A. extension   B. external   C. mother   D. chip

25. All files on the computer are stored in
    A. hard drive   B. RAM
    C. cache   D. associative memory

KEY (CORRECT ANSWERS)

1.	C	11.	B
2.	A	12.	A
3.	B	13.	A
4.	A	14.	A
5.	B	15.	B
6.	B	16.	A
7.	B	17.	B
8.	A	18.	D
9.	B	19.	B
10.	C	20.	A

21. D
22. C
23. B
24. C
25. A

TEST 4

DIRECTIONS: Each question or incomplete statement is followed by several suggested answers or completions. Select the one that BEST answers the question or completes the statement. *PRINT THE LETTER OF THE CORRECT ANSWER IN THE SPACE AT THE RIGHT.*

1. Which one of the following functions are performed by RAM?
   A. Read and Write B. Read
   C. Write D. Update

   1.____

2. _____ is an example of secondary storage.
   A. Diode B. Hard disk C. RAM D. ROM

   2.____

3. USB is a type of _____ storage.
   A. primary B. secondary C. tertiary D. temporary

   3.____

4. MPG file extension is used for _____ files.
   A. video B. audio C. image D. flash

   4.____

5. .exe is an extension for _____ files.
   A. saved B. executable C. system D. software

   5.____

6. Which one of the following is NOT a type of printer?
   A. Inkjet B. Dot matrix C. Laser D. CRT

   6.____

7. _____ sends digital data across a phone line.
   A. Flash B. Modem C. NIC card D. Keyboard

   7.____

8. _____ is a wireless technology used to transfer data among devices over short distances.
   A. USB B. Modem C. Wi-Fi D. Bluetooth

   8.____

9. A user is listening to a song on his computer's music player. He is most likely listening to a(n) _____ file.
   A. .exe B. .mus C. .wav D. .mp3

   9.____

10. PNG is an extension used for _____ files.
    A. audio B. video C. text D. image

    10.____

11. Cache memory is located in the
    A. monitor B. CPU C. DVD D. hard drive

    11.____

12. Computer resolution determines the number of
    A. colors B. pixels C. images D. icons

    12.____

13. _____ is an extension used for images.
    A. GIF B. MP3 C. MPG D. PPT

    13.____

22

14. Which one of the following is NOT an e-mail server?
    A. Gmail B. Yahoo C. Chrome D. Hotmail

15. _____ is an operating system developed by Apple.
    A. Mac IOS B. Linux C. Android D. Windows

16. "What You See Is What You Get" (WYSIWYG) refers to
    A. editing text and graphics for web design
    B. buying a computer at a set price that can't be negotiated
    C. purchasing products as is on websites like Amazon and eBay
    D. printing web pages exactly as they appear on the screen

17. Which one of the following is the BEST option to add a new slide in an existing PowerPoint presentation?
    A. File, add a new slide
    B. File, open
    C. Insert, new slide
    D. File, new

18. _____ is the default setup for page orientation in PowerPoint.
    A. Horizontal B. Vertical C. Landscape D. Portrait

19. Items in a list are typically shown by using
    A. graphics B. bullets C. icons D. markers

20. In PowerPoint, _____ displays only text.
    A. outline view
    B. slide show
    C. print view
    D. slider sorter view

21. In Excel, a cell can be edited by use of
    A. a single click
    B. a double click
    C. the format menu
    D. formulas

22. Formulas are important features of Microsoft
    A. Word B. PowerPoint C. Excel D. Publisher

23. In MS Word, which one of the following is used to underline a text?
    A. Ctrl+I B. Ctrl+B C. Ctrl+U D. Ctrl+P

24. Page color option can be found under the _____ tab.
    A. Page Layout B. Design C. Insert D. View

25. The F1 key typically displays a program's _____ menu.
    A. print
    B. help
    C. tools
    D. task manager

KEY (CORRECT ANSWERS)

1.	A		11.	B
2.	B		12.	B
3.	C		13.	A
4.	A		14.	C
5.	B		15.	A
6.	D		16.	A
7.	B		17.	C
8.	D		18.	C
9.	D		19.	B
10.	D		20.	A

21. A
22. C
23. C
24. B
25. B

EXAMINATION SECTION
TEST 1

DIRECTIONS: Each question or incomplete statement is followed by several suggested answers or completions. Select the one that BEST answers the question or completes the statement. *PRINT THE LETTER OF THE CORRECT ANSWER IN THE SPACE AT THE RIGHT.*

1. Which one of the following is considered a word processor program? 1.____
    A. Microsoft Word
    B. Microsoft Works
    C. Globe Productive
    D. All of the above

2. Basic features of a word processor program include 2.____
    A. page layout option
    B. outline formatting
    C. pre-made templates
    D. all of the above

3. The MOST popular word processor software program is 3.____
    A. Microsoft Word
    B. Microsoft Power Point
    C. Print Shop
    D. Adobe Acrobat

4. Google Docs is appealing to many users because it provides 4.____
    A. image processing
    B. synchronization
    C. voice recognition
    D. multiple languages

5. iPad users generally prefer to use _____ as word processor software. 5.____
    A. Microsoft Word
    B. Textilus
    C. both A and B
    D. none of the above

6. Typeface concerns the _____ of characters. 6.____
    A. shape   B. size   C. type   D. both A and B

7. Identifying the font, alignment and margins is known as 7.____
    A. selecting
    B. formatting
    C. composing
    D. all of the above

8. Indent moves text to the _____ margin. 8.____
    A. both B and C
    B. right of the left
    C. left of the right
    D. none of the above

9. _____ specify areas in the bottom margins of every page. 9.____
    A. Headers
    B. Footers
    C. Indentations
    D. Tabs

10. The _____ feature is used to find words with similar meanings. 10.____
    A. word count
    B. thesaurus
    C. wrap text
    D. all of the above

11. Scrolling moves documents in the
    A. folder
    B. window
    C. trash
    D. all of the above
    11.____

12. Using a(n) _____ assists the user by creating a framework for a new document.
    A. thesaurus
    B. overwrite
    C. template
    D. none of the above
    12.____

13. Which function is used to combine letters to a mailing list?
    A. Insertion
    B. Index generator
    C. Form letter merging
    D. None of the above
    13.____

14. Usually, hyphenation breaks a
    A. line
    B. word
    C. two characters
    D. all of the above
    14.____

15. Substitution of new text for old by typing old text is known as
    A. overstriking
    B. insertion
    C. formatting
    D. both A and B
    15.____

16. Standard documents could be built up by using
    A. auto-formatting
    B. templates
    C. boilerplates
    D. all of the above
    16.____

17. Pagination and page numbering are _____ functions.
    A. identical
    B. different
    C. design
    D. none of the above
    17.____

18. Footnote and _____ work together.
    A. pagination
    B. page number
    C. overstriking
    D. both A and B
    18.____

19. Indents are different from
    A. primary margins
    B. secondary margins
    C. both A and B
    D. none of the above
    19.____

20. Standard blocks of text which appear at the start of the page are known as
    A. header
    B. footer
    C. both A and B
    D. none of the above
    20.____

21. File management capabilities of word processor include
    A. create
    B. delete
    C. search
    D. all of the above
    21.____

22. The word processor can customize which one of the following? 22.____
    A. Typeface
    B. Footnotes
    C. Cross reference
    D. All of the above

23. _____ is a character or word that signifies a sequence of commands. 23.____
    A. Macro   B. Word Wrap
    C. Overstriking   D. All of the above

24. All files with similar data format are handled by using which one of the 24.____
    following functions?
    A. Merges   B. Macros
    C. Cross reference   D. Both A and B

25. Thesaurus allows formatting in _____ documents at a time. 25.____
    A. single   B. two
    C. more than two   D. all of the above

KEY (CORRECT ANSWERS)

1.	D		11.	B
2.	D		12.	C
3.	A		13.	C
4.	B		14.	B
5.	B		15.	A
6.	A		16.	C
7.	B		17.	B
8.	B		18.	A
9.	B		19.	A
10.	B		20.	C

21. D
22. D
23. A
24. A
25. C

TEST 2

DIRECTIONS: Each question or incomplete statement is followed by several suggested answers or completions. Select the one that BEST answers the question or completes the statement. *PRINT THE LETTER OF THE CORRECT ANSWER IN THE SPACE AT THE RIGHT.*

1. Apple has replaced simple text by _____ word processor program.
   A. Text Edit
   B. Textilus
   C. Microsoft Word
   D. all of the above

   1._____

2. Which one of the following is MOST compatible with Microsoft Word?
   A. King Soft Office Writer
   B. Pages
   C. TextEdit
   D. All of the above

   2._____

3. _____ opens up emails received in any format.
   A. Textilus
   B. TextEdits
   C. King Soft Office Writer
   D. All of the above

   3._____

4. Pages works for _____ users in a variety of ways.
   A. Windows
   B. IPad
   C. IPhone
   D. all of the above

   4._____

5. iCloud is used to access files with
   A. Textilus
   B. Pages
   C. Microsoft Word
   D. none of the above

   5._____

6. Synonyms for selected words are also searched by
   A. Overwrite
   B. Thesaurus
   C. Auto Search
   D. all of the above

   6._____

7. Orientation is a property of _____ function.
   A. Print
   B. Design
   C. both A and B
   C. none of the above

   7._____

8. Which one of the following is considered as graphics?
   A. Sketches
   B. All visual elements
   C. Images
   D. All of the above

   8._____

9. The _____ menu helps in switching between multiple files.
   A. Main
   B. Windows
   C. File
   D. none of the above

   9._____

10. Tab helps in the indentation of
    A. paragraphs
    B. lists
    C. both A and B
    D. none of the above

    10._____

11. _____ automatically corrects spelling mistakes.
    A. Word Wrap   B. AutoCorrect
    C. Spell Checker   D. All of the above

12. _____ connects the user to the document on the internet.
    A. Hyperlink   B. Bookmark
    C. Wizard   D. All of the above

13. A wizard is considered as a _____ file with prompt display.
    A. system   B. program
    C. help   D. none of the above

14. Word processing software works for
    A. business   B. education
    C. entertainment   D. all of the above

15. A word processor software must be
    A. easy to understand   B. user friendly
    C. advanced   D. all of the above

16. Quick formatting in Microsoft Word is displayed in the
    A. main menu   B. file menu
    C. semicolon   D. all of the above

17. Decimal alignment is considered as positioning of columns of numbers with the decimal points _____ aligned.
    A. vertically   B. horizontally
    C. straight   D. both A and B

18. _____ automatically changes the text of line if the length is specified.
    A. Autoformat   B. Word Count
    C. Word Wrap   D. None of the above

19. Which function is used to automatically align text?
    A. Justification   B. Indentation
    C. Both A and B   D. None of the above

20. _____ is referred to as re-alignment of text to new margin and tab settings.
    A. Alignment   B. Adjustment
    C. Both A and B   D. None of the above

21. Centering puts _____ on line.
    A. text   B. word
    C. both A and B   D. character

22. Insertion of text _____ existing text.
    A. deletes   B. updates
    C. replaces   D. all of the above

23. _____ is automatic division of a document into pages of specified numbers of lines.
    A. Boilerplate
    B. Overstriking
    C. Pagination
    D. All of the above

24. Which one of the following is TRUE for rich text format?
    A. Removes formatting commands
    B. Formats text
    C. Deletes duplicate text
    D. Both A and B

25. Auto sequential numbering is performed by
    A. footer
    B. header
    C. pagination
    D. all of the above

KEY (CORRECT ANSWERS)

1.	A		11.	B
2.	A		12.	A
3.	C		13.	C
4.	D		14.	D
5.	B		15.	D
6.	B		16.	A
7.	A		17.	A
8.	D		18.	C
9.	B		19.	A
10.	C		20.	B

21.	A
22.	B
23.	C
24.	A
25.	C

TEST 3

DIRECTIONS: Each question or incomplete statement is followed by several suggested answers or completions. Select the one that BEST answers the question or completes the statement. *PRINT THE LETTER OF THE CORRECT ANSWER IN THE SPACE AT THE RIGHT.*

1. Microsoft Works has similarities with
   A. Microsoft Excel
   B. Microsoft Office
   C. Microsoft Word
   D. all of the above

   1.____

2. Basically, a word processor program is a replacement of
   A. manual work
   B. typewriter
   C. both A and B
   D. none of the above

   2.____

3. Which one of the following is NOT a word processor software?
   A. Dark Room
   B. IWork
   C. ABI World
   D. None of the above

   3.____

4. Google Doc uses cloud storage to access files from _____ computers.
   A. single
   B. multiple
   C. neighbor
   D. none of the above

   4.____

5. _____ is an example of an online word processor.
   A. Text Edit
   B. Google Doc
   C. Microsoft Word
   D. All of the above

   5.____

6. Which one of the following is NOT an open source software?
   A. Google Doc
   B. Open Office Writer
   C. Both A and B
   D. None of the above

   6.____

7. Working on multiple operating systems is an important characteristic of
   A. ABI World
   B. Dark Room
   C. Open Office Writer
   D. all of the above

   7.____

8. Clip Art is a collection of _____ which can be inserted into a document.
   A. text files
   B. image files
   C. templates
   D. all of the above

   8.____

9. _____ is a distinctive part of memory which holds the contents temporarily during cut or copy functions.
   A. Clipboard
   B. Macro
   C. Template
   D. All of the above

   9.____

10. Using personal computers to format and produce documents, flyers, letters, reports, and newsletters with the help of graphics is known as
    A. formatting
    B. desktop publishing
    C. editing
    D. all of the above

    10.____

11. Which one of the following is a complimentary close?
    A. Sincerely   B. Truly
    C. Cordially   D. All of the above   11._____

12. Which one of the following is compressed format for images?
    A. GIF   B. JPEG
    C. PNG   D. All of the above   12._____

13. _____ display the relationship between two or more sets of numbers to each other.
    A. Sketches   B. Graphs
    C. Images   D. All of the above   13._____

14. Which one of the following is referred to as an illustration?
    A. Clip Art   B. Graphic
    C. Drawing   D. All of the above   14._____

15. _____ is a formatting feature in which all lines are indented excluding the very first line.
    A. Hanging indent   B. Indent
    C. Margins   D. None of the above   15._____

16. Landscape and Portrait are properties of
    A. page layout   B. design
    C. formatting   D. all of the above   16._____

17. _____ comprises a company's name, address, phone number, and email address.
    A. Letterhead   B. Template
    C. Visiting card   D. All of the above   17._____

18. Bibliography is managed under the _____ tab in Microsoft Office.
    A. Reference   B. Mailing
    C. Design   D. both A and B   18._____

19. Mailings in Microsoft Word concerns
    A. envelopes   B. labels
    C. recipients   D. all of the above   19._____

20. Which one of the following is the MOST common problem with word processor software?
    A. Formatting   B. Version compatibility
    C. Text type   D. None of the above   20._____

21. In word processor software, the Enter key creates
    A. a new paragraph   B. a blank line
    C. breaks in existing paragraph   D. all of the above   21._____

22. Block is referred to as a collection of
    A. words
    B. characters
    C. lines
    D. all of the above

23. Hanging is a type of
    A. margin
    B. indent
    C. alignment
    D. none of the above

24. _____ is included in paragraph alignment.
    A. Justified
    B. Indent
    C. Hanging
    D. Both A and B

25. Inherit property is applied to every _____ when the Enter key is pressed.
    A. paragraph
    B. line
    C. word
    D. all of the above

KEY (CORRECT ANSWERS)

1.	B		11.	D
2.	B		12.	A
3.	D		13.	B
4.	B		14.	D
5.	B		15.	A
6.	A		16.	A
7.	C		17.	A
8.	B		18.	A
9.	A		19.	D
10.	B		20.	B

21. D
22. D
23. B
24. A
25. D

TEST 4

DIRECTIONS: Each question or incomplete statement is followed by several suggested answers or completions. Select the one that BEST answers the question or completes the statement. *PRINT THE LETTER OF THE CORRECT ANSWER IN THE SPACE AT THE RIGHT.*

1. The very first major WYSIWYG is
   A. Ami Pro
   B. Open Office Writer
   C. none of the above
   D. both A and B

   1.____

2. Which one of the following is NOT a word processor?
   A. Open Office Writer
   B. La Tex
   C. Zoho Writer
   D. None of the above

   2.____

3. Zoho Writer has similarities with
   A. Ami Pro
   B. Google Doc
   C. TextEdit
   D. none of the above

   3.____

4. Word processor software is supposed to create
   A. presentations
   B. reports
   C. memos
   D. both B and C

   4.____

5. The best features of Zoho Writer include
   A. templates
   B. integration
   C. free space
   D. all of the above

   5.____

6. Word Graph is a word processor software which facilitates
   A. spell check
   B. PDF creation
   C. track changes
   D. all of the above

   6.____

7. Which one of the following is NOT a well-known word processor?
   A. TextEdit
   B. Word Graph
   C. Abi Word
   D. None of the above

   7.____

8. Which one of the following is CORRECT for an Abi word processor?
   A. Wide range of words
   B. Spell checker
   C. Mail merge
   D. All of the above

   8.____

9. _____ offers insertion of rich media files.
   A. Open Office Writer
   B. Microsoft Office
   C. Google Doc
   D. None of the above

   9.____

10. The WORST aspect of Google Doc is
    A. less storage
    B. compatibility
    C. connectivity to the internet
    D. all of the above

    10.____

11. _____ is comprised of rows and columns and is used to display information.
    A. Tabulation
    B. Table
    C. Alt+Space
    D. All of the above

    11._____

12. Endnote is another name for
    A. footnote
    B. footer
    C. signatures
    D. all of the above

    12._____

13. Word Wrap forces all text to fit within the defined
    A. margin
    B. indent
    C. block
    D. none of the above

    13._____

14. Features such as bold, italics, underline, and regular are considered as
    A. typestyles
    B. typeface
    C. type size
    D. all of the above

    14._____

15. The signature line is especially added to
    A. every document
    B. formal document
    C. sending document
    D. both A and B

    15._____

16. The greeting of the letter is known as
    A. guide word
    B. salutation
    C. address word
    D. all of the above

    16._____

17. _____ is the angle of the characters in a font.
    A. Posture
    B. Style
    C. Typeface
    D. None of the above

    17._____

18. Orientation is concerned with the _____ setup of the page.
    A. horizontal
    B. vertical
    C. both A and B
    D. none of the above

    18._____

19. _____ is a form of written communication within the same company which comprises guide words as heading.
    A. Memorandum
    B. Letterhead
    C. Template
    D. None of the above

    19._____

20. In word processing, the context symbol is referred to as a
    A. character
    B. letter
    C. both A and B
    D. none of the above

    20._____

21. The ruler helps to set which one of the following?
    A. Indent
    B. Margin
    C. Elements
    D. All of the above

    21._____

22. The gutter is the area between two adjacent _____ within a document.
    A. columns
    B. lines
    C. paragraphs
    D. all of the above

    22._____

23. Mail Merge uses _____ to create separate copies of a document for multiple people in Microsoft Word.   23._____
    A. primary document
    B. data document
    C. both A and B
    D. none of the above

24. In Microsoft Word, the overview of the prepared document could be better seen through   24._____
    A. Preview
    B. Print Preview
    C. Review
    D. both A and B

25. In word processor software, fonts are categorized into   25._____
    A. mono-spaced fonts
    B. proportional fonts
    C. both A and B
    D. none of the above

KEY (CORRECT ANSWERS)

1.	A	11.	A
2.	D	12.	A
3.	B	13.	A
4.	D	14.	A
5.	D	15.	C
6.	D	16.	B
7.	C	17.	A
8.	D	18.	C
9.	A	19.	A
10.	C	20.	A

21.	D
22.	A
23.	C
24.	B
25.	C

EXAMINATION SECTION
TEST 1

DIRECTIONS: Each question or incomplete statement is followed by several suggested answers or completions. Select the one that BEST answers the question or completes the statement. *PRINT THE LETTER OF THE CORRECT ANSWER IN THE SPACE AT THE RIGHT.*

1. Cardinality in a relational model refers to numbers of
    A. tuples   B. attributes   C. tables   D. constraints

2. The "AS" clause in SQL is used for which operation?
    A. Selection   B. Rename   C. Join   D. Projection

3. Database code is written in
    A. HLL   B. DML   C. DDL   D. DCL

4. In a hierarchical model, records are organized in
    A. graph   B. list   C. links   D. tree

5. In the entity integrity, the primary key has the value
    A. not null
    B. null
    C. both null and not null
    D. any value

6. The tuple relational calculus P1®P2 stands for
    A. ¬P1 Ú P2   B. P1 Ú P2   C. P1 Ù P2   D. P1 Ù¬P2

7. The method of key transformation is known as
    A. direct   B. hash   C. random   D. sequential

8. The file organization with fast access to any arbitrary record of a file is
    A. ordered file
    B. unordered file
    C. hashed file
    D. B-tree

9. In E-R diagram attributed is symbolized by
    A. ellipse
    B. dashed ellipse
    C. rectangle
    D. triangle

10. The operator used to compare a value to a list of literal values is
    A. BETWEEN   B. ANY   C. IN   D. ALL

11. B-tree of order m has maximum children of
    A. m   B. m+1   C. m-1   D. m/2

12. The function that divides one numeric expression by another and returns the remainder is
    A. POWER   B. MOD   C. ROUND   D. REMAINDER

13. A reflexive association is drawn by
    A. a line
    B. small open diamond
    B. small closed diamond
    D. small triangle at the end of a line

14. The special association that indicates multiple textbooks with a course is _____ association.
    A. aggregation
    B. generalization
    C. n-ary
    D. reflexive

15. In a reflexive association, one class is
    A. broken down into special cases
    B. combined with multiple other classes
    C. combined with one other class
    D. linked back to itself

16. The technique of defining common properties or functions in the higher class and then modifying them in the lower classes is called
    A. inheritance
    B. polymorphism
    C. reflexive
    D. transformance

17. Hiding manager's information from the employees is data hiding at
    A. conceptual level
    B. physical level
    C. external level
    D. none of the above

18. Versatile report provides
    A. columnar totals
    B. subtotals
    C. calculations
    D. all of the above

19. A locked file is
    A. accessed by one user
    B. modified by users having passwords
    C. used to hide sensitive information
    D. both B and C

20. The SQL command that modifies the rows of tables is known as
    A. update   B. insert   C. browse   D. append

21. Which one is NOT an aggregate function?
    A. AVG   B. SUM   C. UPPER   D. MAX

22. In replacing the relation section with some other relation, the initial step is
    A. delete section
    B. drop section
    C. delete from section
    D. replace section with new table

23. Which is NOT a relational database?
    A. dBase IV
    B. 4th Dimension
    C. FoxPro
    D. Reflex

24. A grouped report is a type of report
    A. generated by the Report Wizard
    B. that presents records sorted in ascending or descending order as you specify
    C. that displays data grouped by fields you specify
    D. none of the above

25. The output of (100202,Drake,Biology,30000) is
    A. row(s) inserted
    B. error in ID of insert
    C. error in name of insert
    D. error in salary of the insert

KEY (CORRECT ANSWERS)

1. A
2. B
3. C
4. D
5. A

6. B
7. B
8. C
9. B
10. A

11. A
12. B
13. B
14. D
15. D

16. B
17. C
18. D
19. A
20. A

21. C
22. B
23. D
24. C
25. B

TEST 2

DIRECTIONS: Each question or incomplete statement is followed by several suggested answers or completions. Select the one that BEST answers the question or completes the statement. *PRINT THE LETTER OF THE CORRECT ANSWER IN THE SPACE AT THE RIGHT.*

1. The name of a procedural language is
   - A. domain relational calculus
   - B. tuple relational calculus
   - C. relational algebra
   - D. query language

2. The statement Select* from employee is
   - A. DML
   - B. DDL
   - C. View
   - D. Integrity constraint

3. The Delete from r; r-relation will
   - A. remove relation
   - B. clear relation entries
   - C. delete fields
   - D. delete rows

4. The embedded SQL in COBOL is
   - A. EXEC SQL;
   - B. EXEC SQL END-EXEC
   - C. EXEC SQL
   - D. EXEC SQL END EXEC;

5. Protocols that ensure conflict safety from deadlocks are
   - A. two-phase locking protocol
   - B. time-stamp ordering protocol
   - C. graph based protocol
   - D. both A and B above

6. To reduce the process time of remote backup, we use
   - A. flags
   - B. breakpoints
   - C. redo points
   - D. checkpoints

7. Sort and Filter group commands are in the _____ ribbon.
   - A. Home   B. Create   C. Tools   D. Fields

8. The options Relationship and SQL Server are placed in the _____ tab.
   - A. External Data
   - B. Database Tools
   - C. Create
   - D. Home

9. You cannot drop a table if a Drop Table has a constraint of the _____ key.
   - A. local   B. primary   C. composite   D. foreign

10. Transaction can persist crashes by using the property of
    - A. atomicity
    - B. durability
    - C. isolation
    - D. all of the above

11. Integrity constraints are defined in the language
    - A. DDL Right
    - B. DCL
    - C. DML
    - D. none of the above

2 (#2)

12. A group of commands collectively performing a function is
    A. procedure
    B. transaction right!
    C. query
    D. function

13. Poor administration of data leads to
    A. same data entity with single definition
    B. familiarity of existing data
    C. data elements missing
    D. all of the above

14. The intrusion detection system does not perform
    A. identification of hacking attempt into a system
    B. monitoring transfer of packets over the network
    C. transmitting the message packets to destination
    D. establishing deception systems to trap hackers

15. Hypertext Transfer Protocol (HTTP) defines the
    A. protocol to copy files between computers
    B. transfer protocol to transfer web pages to a browser
    C. database access protocol for SQL statements
    D. hardware/software protocol that limits access to company data

16. A CASE SQL statement defines
    A. an IF-THEN-ELSE in SQL
    B. a loop in SQL
    C. data definition in SQL
    D. all of the above

17. Routines and triggers define
    A. procedural code
    B. a call to operate
    C. automatic run
    D. storage in the database

18. To join tables, we take the approach of
    A. subqueries
    B. union join
    C. natural join
    D. all of the above

19. Backward recovery defines
    A. before-images applied to the database
    B. after-images applied to the database
    C. after-images and before-images applied to the database
    D. switching to an existing copy of the database

20. Locking may cause
    A. erroneous updates
    B. deadlock
    C. versioning
    D. all of the above

21. After a system failure, you recover a database through
    A. rollback
    B. rollforward
    C. switch to duplicate database
    D. reprocess transactions

22. Read-only databases are _____ updated.
    A. always   B. commonly   C. seldom   D. never

23. In order to secure a database, an administrative policy must consider
    A. authentication policies
    B. limiting access to only authorized people
    C. ensuring appropriate response rates are in external maintenance agreements
    D. all of the above

24. Data management technology does not include
    A. relational   B. rational
    C. object-oriented   D. dimensional

25. SQL INSERT statement defines
    A. rows modified according to criteria only
    B. mass of rows which cannot be copied from one table to another only
    C. rows inserted into a table only one at a time
    D. rows inserted into a table one at a time or in groups

KEY (CORRECT ANSWERS)

1.	C		11.	A
2.	A		12.	B
3.	C		13.	C
4.	B		14.	C
5.	B		15.	B
6.	D		16.	A
7.	A		17.	A
8.	B		18.	D
9.	D		19.	A
10.	B		20.	B

21. C
22. D
23. D
24. B
25. D

TEST 3

DIRECTIONS: Each question or incomplete statement is followed by several suggested answers or completions. Select the one that BEST answers the question or completes the statement. *PRINT THE LETTER OF THE CORRECT ANSWER IN THE SPACE AT THE RIGHT.*

1. Which one is NOT a component of a database?
    A. User data   B. Metadata   C. Reports   D. Indexes

2. The commercial website Amazon.com is an example of _____ database application.
    A. single-user
    B. multi-user
    C. e-commerce
    D. data mining

3. Which of the following products was the FIRST to implement true relational algebra in a PC DBMS?
    A. IDMS   B. Oracle   C. dBase-II   D. R:base

4. SQL stands for _____ Language.
    A. Structured Query
    B. Sequential Query
    C. Structured Question
    D. Sequential Question

5. DBMS function is not used to
    A. create and process forms
    B. create databases
    C. process data
    D. administer databases

6. Which function assists people to keep track of their things?
    A. Database   B. Table   C. Instance   D. Relationship

7. In an ODBC environment, a mediator between application and the DBMS drivers is
    A. data source
    B. driver
    C. driver manager
    D. OLE DB

8. An Enterprise Resource Planning application is a(n) _____ database application.
    A. single-user
    B. multi-user
    C. e-commerce
    D. data mining

9. The use of ID-dependent entities defines
    A. association relationships only
    B. multi-valued attributes only
    C. archetype/instance relationships only
    D. all of the above use ID dependent entities

10. The entity identifier in a table is
    A. foreign key
    B. main attribute
    C. primary key
    D. identity key

11. Which is FALSE for surrogate keys?
    A. They are short
    B. They are fixed
    C. They have meaning to the user
    D. They are numeric

12. Minimum cardinalities for every relationship is
    A. two
    B. three
    C. four
    D. six

13. VPD provides authorization, and the mechanism is called
    A. row-level authorization
    B. column-level authorization
    C. row-type authentication
    D. authorization security

14. ON UPDATE CASCADE ensures
    A. normalization
    B. data integrity
    C. materialized views
    D. all of the above

15. SQL for an index is
    A. CREATE INDEX ID;
    B. CHANGE INDEX ID;
    C. ADD INDEX ID;
    D. REMOVE INDEX ID;

16. The sub-query bracket of an SQL SELECT statement is
    A. Braces – {...}
    B. CAPITAL LETTERS
    C. parenthesis – (...)
    D. brackets – [...]

17. Five built-in functions provided by SQL are
    A. COUNT, SUM, AVG, MAX, MIN
    B. SUM, AVG, MIN, MAX, MULT
    C. SUM, AVG, MULT, DIV, MIN
    D. SUM, AVG, MIN, MAX, NAME

18. The Microsoft Access wildcards are
    A. asterisk (*); percent sign (%)
    B. percent sign (%); underscore (_)
    C. underscore (_); question mark (?)
    D. question mark (?); asterisk (*)

19. The function used to sort rows in SQL is
    A. SORT BY
    B. ALIGN BY
    C. ORDER BY
    D. GROUP BY

20. EXISTS keyword defines
    A. only one row in the sub-query meets the condition
    B. all rows in the sub-query fail the condition
    C. both A and B
    D. none of the above

21. In SQL Server 2000, the parameters used in stored procedures are indicated with
    A. #
    B. %
    C. &
    D. @

22. Trigger supported by SQL Server is
    A. INSTEAD OF only
    B. AFTER only
    C. BEFORE only
    D. INSTEAD OF and AFTER only

3 (#3)

23. Which function in SQL Server 2000 tracks copy of changes since the last backup in the database? 23.____
    A. Complete backup
    B. Transaction log
    C. Differential backup
    D. None of the above

24. The transaction log defines the ____ of a record. 24.____
    A. before-image
    B. after-image
    C. before and after-image
    D. essential data

25. Database is recovered by 25.____
    A. rollback
    B. rollforward
    C. switch to duplicate database
    D. reprocess transactions

KEY (CORRECT ANSWERS)

1.	C		11.	C
2.	C		12.	D
3.	D		13.	A
4.	A		14.	B
5.	A		15.	A
6.	A		16.	C
7.	C		17.	A
8.	B		18.	D
9.	D		19.	C
10.	C		20.	A

21. D
22. D
23. C
24. D
25. C

TEST 4

DIRECTIONS: Each question or incomplete statement is followed by several suggested answers or completions. Select the one that BEST answers the question or completes the statement. *PRINT THE LETTER OF THE CORRECT ANSWER IN THE SPACE AT THE RIGHT.*

1. A relational database includes a collection of
   A. tables B. fields C. records D. keys

2. A domain is said to be atomic if elements are
   A. different B. indivisible C. constant D. divisible

3. The statement Course(course_id,sec_id,semester) course_id,sec_id and semester are defined as
   A. relations, attribute
   B. attributes, relation
   C. tuple, relation
   D. tuple, attributes

4. Each entity has a descriptive property called
   A. entity B. attribute C. relation D. model

5. The structure of the relation, deleting relation, and relating schemas is defined in
   A. DML (Data Manipulation Language)
   B. DDL (Data Definition Language)
   C. Query
   D. Relational Schema

6. To query information and to insert tuples, delete tuples, and modify tuples we use
   A. DML (Data Manipulation Language)
   B. DDL (Data Definition Language)
   C. Query
   D. Relational Schema

7. Which function is used to remove a relation from an SQL database?
   A. Delete B. Purge C. Remove D. Drop Table

8. Insert into instructor values (10211,'Smith','Biology',66000); defines
   A. Query B. DML C. Relational D. DDL

9. To append two strings, we use operator
   A. & B. % C. || D. _

10. In the DBMS environment, Date format is
    A. mm/dd/yy B. yyyy/mm/dd C. dd/mm/yy D. yy/dd/mm

11. SQL store movie and image files by data type:
    A. clob B. blob C. binary D. image

12. Hashing search defines _____ time.
    A. O(1) B. O(n2) C. O(log n) D. O(n log n)

13. Key value pairs defines
    A. hash tables B. heaps C. both A and B D. skip list

14. Breadth First Search is
    A. binary trees
    B. stacks
    C. graphs
    D. both A and C above

15. We identify deleted records by _____ bitmap.
    A. existence B. current C. final D. deleted

16. The oldest database model is
    A. relational B. deductive C. physical D. network

17. Snapshot isolation defines
    A. concurrency-control
    B. concurrency-allowance
    C. redirection
    D. repetition-allowance

18. A condition in SQL is
    A. join in SQL
    B. join condition
    C. both of the above
    D. none of the above

19. The operation allowed in a join view is
    A. UPDATE
    B. INSERT
    C. DELETE
    D. all of the above

20. Concurrency control on B+ trees is used to
    A. remove unwanted data
    B. easily add the index elements
    C. maintain accuracy of index
    D. all of the above

21. The protocol locking while crabbing goes
    A. down the tree and back up
    B. up the tree and back down
    C. down the tree and releases
    D. up the tree and releases

22. To reduce overhead and retrieve records from storage we use
    A. logs
    B. log buffer
    C. medieval space
    D. lower records

23. The space on disk allocated by the operating system for storing virtual-memory pages are called
    A. latches
    B. swap space
    C. dirty block
    D. none of the above

24. In two-factor authentication, the users can face an attack called   24._____
    A. radiant   B. cross attack
    C. scripting   D. man-in-the-middle

25. The attack that force an application to execute an SQL query is called   25._____
    A. SQL injection   B. SQL   C. direct   D. application

KEY (CORRECT ANSWERS)

1. A
2. B
3. B
4. B
5. B

6. A
7. D
8. B
9. C
10. B

11. B
12. A
13. A
14. C
15. A

16. D
17. A
18. B
19. D
20. C

21. A
22. B
23. B
24. D
25. A

EXAMINATION SECTION
TEST 1

DIRECTIONS: Each question or incomplete statement is followed by several suggested answers or completions. Select the one that BEST answers the question or completes the statement. *PRINT THE LETTER OF THE CORRECT ANSWER IN THE SPACE AT THE RIGHT.*

1. A hard disk is divided into tracks which are further subdivided into
   A. vectors
   B. partitions
   C. sectors
   D. none of the above

   1.____

2. After boot up, what is the first location from which the computer instructions are available?
   A. CPU
   B. RAM
   C. ROM
   D. ROM BIOS

   2.____

3. What is the standard which is used for parallel communications?
   A. CAT5
   B. IEEE 802.11
   C. IEEE 1284
   D. RS232

   3.____

4. If you have a maintenance package which identifies several field replaceable units (FRU's), these can be used to resolve the problem. What will you do after the power has been turned off?
   A. Replace all the parts at once.
   B. Replace the parts indicated, one by one, in a sequence which is recommended until the issue is solved.
   C. Consult your administrator.
   D. Look for the solution of this problem online.

   4.____

5. Which of the following conditions is used to transmit two packets over a medium at the same time?
   A. Contention
   B. Collision
   C. Synchronous
   D. None of the above

   5.____

6. What is the main purpose of an operating system?
   A. Make the computer user friendly.
   B. Make most efficient use of computer hardware.
   C. Make the programs run faster.
   D. Make the accessibility much easier.

   6.____

7. What is the tool used for testing parallel and serial ports?
   A. Wrap plugs
   B. High voltage probe
   C. Connecting cable
   D. None of the above

   7.____

8. Which of the following operating systems does not depict the best implementation of multitasking?
   A. Windows XP   B. MS-DOS
   C. Windows 7   D. Windows 8

9. What is the 25-pin female connector at the back of your computer?
   A. Serial port   B. Parallel port
   C. USB port   D. None of the above

10. Which one of the following is the MOST suitable option after you have installed new drivers on your computer?
    A. Shutdown   B. Hibernate   C. Sleep   D. Restart

11. Which one of the following is NOT an application software?
    A. Picassa   B. Photoshop   C. Windows XP   D. Skype

12. Which one of the following devices can be shared over a network?
    A. Printer   B. Keyword
    C. Word files   D. Email addresses

13. Which of these ports do NOT exist in a laptop?
    A. Serial   B. USB
    C. Parallel   D. None of the above

14. One byte contains _____ bits.
    A. 4   B. 8   C. 10   D. 12

15. One nible contains _____ bits.
    A. 2   B. 3   C. 4   D. 6

16. Which one of the following devices is used for data processing?
    A. RAM   B. ROM   C. Monitor   D. CPU

17. The FIRST thing which needs to be done in order to check if the printer is damaged or not is
    A. run the diagnostics
    B. check the connecting cables
    C. remove the outer box and check for any sort of physical damage
    D. attach it to the computer and print something

18. The command used to view the version of the operating system is
    A. Version   B. Ver   C. V*   D. V.

19. If the power supply is cut off, which of these data will be erased?
    A. EPROM   B. RAM
    C. USB   D. None of the above

20. What part of 192.168.10.51 is the Network ID, assuming a default subnet mask?
    A. 192
    B. 191.168.10
    C. 0.0.0.5
    D. 51

    20._____

21. Which one of these can help in reducing TCP/IP configuration problems?
    A. WINS Proxy
    B. DHCP Server
    C. PDC
    D. None of the above

    21._____

22. Which device of the computer operation dispenses with the use of the keyboard?
    A. Light Pen
    B. Mouse
    C. Touch
    D. All of the above

    22._____

23. In order to establish a top-to-bottom relationship among the items in a database, we can use a _____ schema.
    A. hierarchical
    B. network
    C. relational
    D. all of the above

    23._____

24. Linux is a(n) _____ operating system.
    A. Mac
    B. Windows
    C. Open Source
    D. all of the above

    24._____

25. DDL stands for
    A. Data Design Language
    B. Data Definition Language
    C. Design Detailed Language
    D. Developed Design Language

    25._____

KEY (CORRECT ANSWERS)

1.	C	11.	C
2.	D	12.	A
3.	C	13.	D
4.	B	14.	B
5.	B	15.	C
6.	B	16.	A
7.	A	17.	C
8.	B	18.	B
9.	B	19.	B
10.	D	20.	B

21.	B
22.	B
23.	A
24.	C
25.	B

TEST 2

DIRECTIONS: Each question or incomplete statement is followed by several suggested answers or completions. Select the one that BEST answers the question or completes the statement. *PRINT THE LETTER OF THE CORRECT ANSWER IN THE SPACE AT THE RIGHT.*

1. Which of these files is MOST essential in every computer?
   A. .sys
   B. .com
   C. .exe
   D. All of the above

2. Which command allows you to reduce fragments of file and optimize the performance of disk?
   A. Scandisk   B. Defrag   C. Diskcomp   D. Chkdsk

3. Which of the following is a spreadsheet package?
   A. Excel
   B. Lotus
   C. Quattro Pro
   D. All of the above

4. In MS-DOS, which one of the following is used to create a directory?
   A. MakeDirectory   B. MD   C. Mkdir   D. CD

5. The MS-DOS command can be used for printing any document.
   A. True
   B. False

6. Data can be stored in
   A. USB
   B. floppy
   C. CD
   D. all of the above

7. The various cards in the computer require _____ voltage to function.
   A. AC
   B. DC
   C. fluctuating current
   D. none of the above

8. What does FAT stand for?
   A. File Allocation Terminal
   B. File Allocation Table
   C. Fast Allocation Table
   D. File Accessing Table

9. The name of the printed circuit board on the CPU is called
   A. motherboard
   B. PC card
   C. microcontroller
   D. ROM

10. Another name of the LCB monitor is
    A. CRT   B. TFT   C. TFF   D. CRC

52

11. In order to determine that a particular ribbon cable needs to be used for connecting with a floppy drive, the BEST way is to check if the
    A. ribbon has a twist
    B. color of the ribbon is blue
    C. ribbon has a black dotted line along the sides
    D. ribbon is colored red

12. Another name for the hard drive is _____ drive.
    A. Wisley   B. Winchester   C. Internal   D. Fragmented

13. The type of CD ROM which should be used in order to write and rewrite data is
    A. CD-R
    B. CD-RW
    C. CD
    D. all of the above

14. SMPS stands for
    A. Simple Mode Power System
    B. Simple Median Power Stream
    C. Switch Mode Power Supply
    D. Simple Mode Power Supply

15. Which of the following is NOT a type of motherboard expansion slot?
    A. ISA   B. PCI   C. ATX   D. PLC

16. Fragmentation of data on a computer hard disk causes it to work faster than before.
    A. False   B. True

17. The card which is used to control the motor in the hard disk and is also responsible for controlling the read/write operation is called the
    A. disc controller card
    B. PLC card
    C. network card
    D. memory cache

18. What is the number of bytes that are held by the sector of a hard disk?
    A. 512   B. 1246   C. 1024   D. 2048

19. The name of the connector that is used to connect the power supply of the power supply of the PC to the hard drive is
    A. Molex   B. Mini-molex   C. P9   D. AT

20. What is the number of pins in DIMM?
    A. 32   B. 72   C. 82   D. 92

21. A computer program that translates one program instruction at a time into machine language is called a(n)
    A. CPU   B. RAM   C. Interpreter   D. ROM

22. Which of the following is NOT a logical database structure?
    A. Tree   B. Relational   C. Network   D. Chain

23. It is the responsibility of the database administrator to 23.____
    A. backup the database   B. monitor performance
    C. design an efficient database D. all of the above

24. The step-by-step instructions that solve a problem are called 24.____
    A. list   B. plan   C. algorithm   D. tasks

25. Transmission speed is slowest in 25.____
    A. coaxial cable   B. fiber optic
    C. microwaves   D. twisted-pair wire

KEY (CORRECT ANSWERS)

1.	D		11.	A
2.	B		12.	B
3.	D		13.	B
4.	C		14.	C
5.	A		15.	C
6.	D		16.	A
7.	B		17.	A
8.	B		18.	C
9.	A		19.	A
10.	B		20.	B

21. C
22. D
23. D
24. C
25. D

TEST 3

DIRECTIONS: Each question or incomplete statement is followed by several suggested answers or completions. Select the one that BEST answers the question or completes the statement. *PRINT THE LETTER OF THE CORRECT ANSWER IN THE SPACE AT THE RIGHT.*

1. OLE stands for
   A. object linking and embedding
   B. open link and embed
   C. objective linking and emulation
   D. object liking and embedding

   1.____

2. Windows _____ supports 64 bit processor.
   A. NT   B. XP   C. 7   D. 98

   2.____

3. What is meant by a workgroup?
   A. Individual computer
   B. Computer in a network
   C. Computer arranged in a room
   D. None of the above

   3.____

4. ISP stands for
   A. intranet service provision
   B. internet service provider
   C. international service provider
   D. internal system provider

   4.____

5. The functionality of a folder is
   A. storing and saving files
   B. deleting files
   C. remaining files
   D. none of the above

   5.____

6. The frames from one LAN can be transmitted to another LAN via the device
   A. router   B. repeater   C. bridge   D. modem

   6.____

7. Which one of the following is built directly on the hardware?
   A. Operating system
   B. Networking system
   C. System software
   D. None of the above

   7.____

8. Which of the following operating systems do you choose to implement a client server network?
   A. Windows NT
   B. Windows 2000
   C. Windows XP
   D. MS-DOS

   8.____

9. Which of the following devices is used for modulation and demodulation?
   A. Gateway
   B. Multiplexer
   C. Modem
   D. None of the above

   9.____

10. Which one of the following is NOT linked with a database?
    A. Form   B. Macro   C. Table   D. Query

    10.____

11. Windows _____ does not have a Start button.
    A. XP   B. 8   C. Vista   D. NT

    11.____

55

12. Which one of the following TCP/IP protocols is used for transferring electronic mail messages from one machine to another?
    A. NMP   B. FTP   C. SMTP   D. RPC

13. A distributed network configuration in which all data/information pass through a central computer is a _____ network.
    A. ring   B. star   C. bus   D. point-to-point

14. HTML stands for
    A. Hypertext Module Language
    B. Hyperlink Module Language
    C. Hypertext Modern Language
    D. none of the above

15. What is the MOST suitable way to organize data in a spreadsheet?
    A. Rows and columns
    B. Patterns
    C. Numbers
    D. None of the above

16. Which of the following parts interprets program instructions and initiates control operations?
    A. Input
    B. Storage unit
    C. Logic unit
    D. Control unit

17. Binary numbers need more places for counting because
    A. they are always big numbers
    B. any number of 0's can be added in front of them
    C. binary base is small
    D. 0's and 1's have to be properly spaced apart

18. The section of the CPU that selects, interprets, and sees to the execution of program instructions is called
    A. memory
    B. register unit
    C. control unit
    D. none of the above

19. The single packet on the data link is called
    A. group   B. block   C. frame   D. path

20. The computer which has been designed to be as compact as possible is called the
    A. mainframe
    B. super computer
    C. micro computer
    D. none of the above

21. What is the BEST way to use to connect to a remote computer?
    A. Diagnostic
    B. Logic circuit
    C. Dial-up
    D. Device

22. Which is the type of RAM used in a PC these days?
    A. DDR SDRAM   B. DDR2   C. DDR   D. DDR1

23. Which of the following is NOT a type of RAM?
    A. DIMM   B. DDR2   C. SIMM   D. ROM

24. Which one of the following disk drives has more storage? 24._____
    A. DVD   B. CD
    C. Floppy drive   D. CD-RW

25. What is the name of the display feature whose highlights are of the screen 25._____
    which requires operator attention?\
    A. Reverse video   B. Pixel
    C. Cursor   D. Touchscreen

KEY (CORRECT ANSWERS)

1.	A	11.	B
2.	D	12.	C
3.	B	13.	B
4.	B	14.	A
5.	A	15.	A
6.	C	16.	D
7.	B	17.	C
8.	B	18.	C
9.	C	19.	C
10.	B	20.	C

21.	C
22.	A
23.	D
24.	A
25.	A

TEST 4

DIRECTIONS: Each question or incomplete statement is followed by several suggested answers or completions. Select the one that BEST answers the question or completes the statement. *PRINT THE LETTER OF THE CORRECT ANSWER IN THE SPACE AT THE RIGHT.*

1. Which of the following operating systems can have the SMALLEST file name?　　1.____
    A. DOS
    B. Windows XP
    C. Windows 99
    C. Windows 7

2. Why is the Radio button used?　　2.____
    A. Selecting single option
    B. Selecting a number of options
    C. This button has no functionality
    D. Turn on the parallel port

3. The Basic Input Output System (BIOS) is present in　　3.____
    A. CPU
    B. memory registers
    C. EPROM
    D. ROM

4. Where are recently deleted files present?　　4.____
    A. My Documents
    B. Recycle Bin
    C. My Computer
    D. Memory cache

5. The layer of a computer system between the user and the hardware is called the　　5.____
    A. application software
    B. system software
    C. operating system
    D. process identifier

6. The command which is used to create a logical drive for a specific location of a disk is　　6.____
    A. Del
    B. Format
    C. Fdisk
    D. Subst

7. What happens during the maintenance phase?　　7.____
    A. System requirements are established.
    B. System analysis is carried out.
    C. Programs are tested
    D. Ongoing systems are maintained and tested.

8. In system analysis decision, trees are used for　　8.____
    A. pictorial depiction of alternate conditions
    B. nodes and branches
    C. consequences of various depicted alternates
    D. all of the above

9. A process is considered as　　9.____
    A. contents of main memory
    B. program in execution
    C. sequence of events
    D. all of the above

10. What is done in inter-process communication?
    A. Allows processes to synchronize activity
    B. Makes use of the internal memory
    C. Used for process communication
    D. None of the above

11. Which of the following is loaded into main memory when the computer is booted?
    A. Internal command instructions
    B. External command instructions
    C. Utility programs
    D. Word processing instructions

12. Which one of the following is an example of a web browser?
    A. Yahoo.com
    B. Windows Explorer
    C. Outlook Express
    D. Google.com

13. The BEST way to connect a computer to another computer in the same room is
    A. coaxial cable
    B. fiber optic cable
    C. dedicated line
    D. none of the above

14. Which one of the following types of channels moves data relatively slowly?
    A. Broadband   B. Wideband   C. Narrowband   D. Voice band

15. Which one of the following is NOT a system tool?
    A. Backing up data
    B. Fragmenting a disk
    C. Scanning for virus
    D. Compiling

16. Is there any difference between search engine and gateway?
    A. Yes
    B. No

17. The average time which is necessary for the correct sector of a disk to arrive at the read/write head is known as
    A. down time
    B. uploading time
    C. seek time
    D. rotational delay

18. ASCII is the short form for American _____ for Information Interchange.
    A. Science Center
    B. Standard Code
    C. Scientific Code
    D. System Code

19. The boundary separating two systems is referred to as
    A. surface
    B. interface
    C. separator
    D. none of the above

20. The type of storage which is used for holding information between steps in its processing is referred to as _____ storage.
    A. internal   B. external   C. primary   D. intermediate

21. A binary system is a system which uses power of
    A. 100   B. 10   C. 2   D. 1

22. The time and date is always displayed on the
    A. system tray
    B. taskbar
    C. menu bar
    D. status bar

23. Which one of the following commands is used in MS-DOS?
    A. CD
    B. MD
    C. MKDIR
    D. All of the above

24. A taskbar is used for
    A. navigating in a program
    B. switching in between programs
    C. closing a program
    D. all of the above

25. Parallel port is also referred to as RS-232.
    A. True
    B. False

KEY (CORRECT ANSWERS)

1.	A	11.	A
2.	A	12.	B
3.	D	13.	A
4.	B	14.	C
5.	C	15.	C
6.	D	16.	A
7.	D	17.	D
8.	B	18.	A
9.	B	19.	B
10.	A	20.	D

21. C
22. A
23. D
24. D
25. B

EXAMINATION SECTION
TEST 1

DIRECTIONS: Each question or incomplete statement is followed by several suggested answers or completions. Select the one that BEST answers the question or completes the statement. *PRINT THE LETTER OF THE CORRECT ANSWER IN THE SPACE AT THE RIGHT.*

1. The internal components of computers run on direct current (DC). A(n) _____ converts the power supply from power companies to suit the internal components.
    A. power supply unit (PSU)
    B. power transformation unit (PTU)
    C. AC-to-DC converter (ADC)
    D. power regulation unit (PRU)

1.____

2. Peripherals are connected to each other through integrated circuits provided on the
    A. central processing unit
    B. arithmetic logic unit
    C. controller unit
    D. motherboard

2.____

3. BIOS stands for
    A. Binary Operating System
    B. Basic Input/Output System
    C. Basic Initial Operating Semantics
    D. Beginner Instructions for Operating Systems

3.____

4. BIOS is stored on
    A. Random Access Memory (RAM)
    B. EPROM
    C. Read Only Memory (ROM)
    D. DIMM

4.____

5. Image scanners and touchpad are both _____ devices.
    A. input   B. output   C. tracking   D. pointing

5.____

6. A video card is also known as a _____ card.
    A. multi IO
    B. graphics
    C. math processing
    D. SCSI

6.____

7. _____ are typically used for creating large-scale maps and architectural drawings.
    A. Tablets   B. Digitizers   C. Plotters   D. Scanners

7.____

8. In some newer systems, BIOS has been replaced by
    A. FDDI   B. DIMM   C. SIMM   D. UEFI

8.____

9. _____ drives are now used instead of hard disk drives (HDD).
    A. Solid state   B. USB flash   C. Nano   D. Optical

9.____

10. As of 2016, the fastest supercomputer in the world is
    A. Sunway Taihulight   B. Univac III
    C. Topacredic China   D. Advac 09

11. Ethernet and audio jack are both examples of
    A. expansion slots   B. output devices
    C. data ports   D. input devices

12. What kind of supported devices attach with each other to minimize cables and attach in a series?
    A. Serial BUS   B. SCSI   C. Ethernet   D. Parallel Ports

13. A network shared printer is not printing the documents sent from the network. Which of the following is the FIRST troubleshooting step to take?
    A. Check printer driver   B. Check printer configuration
    C. Confirm it is online   D. Check the network interface card

14. An operator has been assigned to send a letter to 500 addresses by postal service Which of the following is the BEST method for preparing letters and envelopes (assume the list of addresses is available) at an efficient pace?
    A. Text editor   B. Image processing software
    C. Database software   D. Spreadsheet software
    E. A, C or D

15. An engineering firm makes large maps for its survey-related needs. Which of the following will support the printing of such documents?
    A. Thermal printer   B. Daisywheel printer
    C. Plotter   D. Wide-carriage dot-matrix printer

16. Sports data is updated every few minutes. An operator will keep a record of each shot attempted in a basketball game. What would be the BEST way to perform this task?
    A. Use spreadsheet software like MS Excel
    B. Use dedicated software that records the appropriate data
    C. Manually record the scores and the enter into the computer
    D. Use remote sensors installed on the court

17. A company receives an average of 20 calls per minute from its offshore customers. What software would allow the automated answering process to filter important calls in an efficient way?
    A. TCP   B. CAED   C. IVR   D. CAM

18. A utility customer is surprised to see a telephone bill in her name for $0.00 at her doorstep. Which one of the following could have helped to avoid this error?
    A. Efficient hardware   B. Data storage medium
    C. Application software   D. Inland mailing process

19. An operator claims that he can make a soft copy from a hard copy without retyping. His claim is due to the availability of _____ software.
    A. OCP	B. OCR	C. DHCP	D. DFD

20. Official photographs from company events are growing day by day, which exerts more and more strain on available storage resources. How can the company's available data be stored and retrieved on demand in an organized fashion?
    A. Database application software
    B. Cloud storage
    C. Upgrade system hardware
    D. Upgrade image-processing software

21. Which tool would you use to read a log of events that occurred on the computer?
    A. Event viewer	B. Event logger
    C. Task scheduler	D. Device manager

22. GPU stands for
    A. General Process Uniformity	B. Graphics Processing Unit
    C. Games Processing Unit	D. Gaming Program Unit

23. Your copier makes PDF document scans. What other hardware can possibly generate a copy of a one-page document to be sent through e-mail?
    A. Cellphone with PC access	B. Fax machine
    C. Scanner	D. Thermal printer

24. RFID is used to
    A. gather data
    B. track objects
    C. analyze radio frequencies
    D. control human computer interaction

25. Which of the following is NOT a backup scheme?
    A. Grandfather-father-son	B. Tower of Hanoi
    C. Bubble Out	D. Weighted random distribution

KEY (CORRECT ANSWERS)

1. A
2. D
3. B
4. C
5. A

6. B
7. C
8. D
9. A
10. A

11. C
12. B
13. C
14. E
15. C

16. B
17. C
18. C
19. B
20. A

21. A
22. B
23. A
24. B
25. C

———

TEST 2

DIRECTIONS: Each question or incomplete statement is followed by several suggested answers or completions. Select the one that BEST answers the question or completes the statement. *PRINT THE LETTER OF THE CORRECT ANSWER IN THE SPACE AT THE RIGHT.*

1. We use _____ type for a hexadecimal number.
   A. char B. double C. string D. int

2. _____ numbers use floating point.
   A. Real B. Binary C. Octal D. Decimal

3. int a_ = 014;
   Why is the above block statement NOT correct?
   A. Outside range
   B. Values beginning with 0 are not supported
   C. Identifier is not legal
   D. Wrong combination

4. To deal with text, which of the following is used?
   A. char B. double C. string D. int

5. int a=1, b=2
   int c = ++a+b+++a++;
   What is the correct output?
   A. 5 B. 10 C. 8 D. 6

6. (2016%4) == 0? "leap year" : "year" ;
   Which of the following is the correct output generated?
   A. leap year B. year
   C. syntax error D. runtime error

7. int a = 1;
   int b = 1;
   if(!(true)&&(a++<5)||(b++<-15))
       a+=1;
   b=a;
   if(!(10>12))
       a+=10;
   b=a;
   if(!(a>1)&&((b*=2)>3))
       a+=200;
   System.out.println("a=" + a + "b = "+b);
   Which pair of values below is correct concerning the above block of code?
   A. a=211 b=11 B. a=11 b=11
   C. a=1 b=1 D. Syntax error

8. if(!true||!false)
       System.out.println(true);
   else
       System.out.println(false);
   What is the output generated by the above code snippet?
   A. Prints true   B. Prints false
   C. Program hangs   D. Syntax error

   8.____

9. Objects sharing a memory location are
   A. equal   B. identical   C. duplicate   D. siblings

   9.____

10. Dividing a float value by zero (0) generates
    A. arithmetic exception   B. 0
    C. infinity   D. 1

    10.____

11.

10		20		30	
10	20		30	40	50
10	20		30	50	
40					

11.____

Which is the CORRECT option for the declared multidimensional array as given in the above table?

A. int[][]mazArray = {
            {10,0,20,0,30],
            {10,20,30,40,50],
            {10,20,30,50,0},
            {40}
       };

B. int[][]mazArray = {   {10,20,30,0,0},
                         {10,20,30,40,50},
                         {10,20,30,50,0},
                         {40,0,0,0,0}
       };

C. int[][]mazArray = {   {10,20},
                         {30,10,20,30,40,50},
                         {10,20,30}
       };

D. int[][]mazArray = {
                         {10,20,30},
                         {10,20,30,40,50},
                         {10,20,30,50},
                         {40}
       };

12. Examine this series: 7, 10, , 11, 9, 12, ...
    What number should come next?
    A. 7 B. 10 C. 12 D. 13

13. A program loops indefinitely. What should you press?
    A. ALT Break
    B. CONTROL and C
    C. Escape key
    D. CTRL ALT DEL

14. ```
    int cnt = 1;
    while (cnt<=25)
    {
    System.out.println(cnt);
    Cnt = cnt – 1;
    }
    System.out.println("Done");
    ```
    What output is generated from the above statements?
    A. 1 thru 25 is printed
    B. 25 thru 1 is printed
    C. Syntax error
    D. Counts from 1 backwards and loops infinitely

15. _____ is the process of finding errors and fixing them within a program.
    A. Compiling B. Executing C. Debugging D. Scanning

16. The number of executions of a loop is unknown. What kind of loop should be used?
    A. For Loop B. Switch C. While loop D. Nested IF

17. ```
    marks = Keyboard.readInt();
    while (marks!=-1)
    {
    System.out.println("Net is" + marks);
    marks = Keyboard.readInt();
    ```
    What is the output of the above code?
    A. Marks continuously asked and printed
    B. While loop executes endlessly
    C. "Net is" never reached or printed as it is false from the very beginning
    D. While executed for all values not equal to -1 entered

18. Consider the conditional statements.
    If the condition is true, which one of the following will execute?
    A. If (x<0)a=b*2; y = x; z = a – y
    B. {if(x<0)a=b*2; y = x; z = a – y;}
    C. If {(x<0)a=b*2; y = x; z = a – y;}
    D. If (x<0)   {a=b*2; y = x; z = a – y;}

19. A loop that never ends is called a(n) _____ loop.
    A. while B. recursive C. infinite D. for

20. Which one of the following declares an array of five elements and initializes it with five numbers?
    A. Array a = new Array(5);
    B. int[]a = {23,22,21,20,19};
    C. int a[]= new int[5];
    D. int[5] array;

21. I.   char c1 = 08880;
    II. char c2 = 'name';
    III. char c3 = 0xbfff;
    IV. char c4 = \u001;
    V.   char c5 = '\iface';
    VI. char c6 = '\uface';
    Which three are valid character type declarations?
    A. I, II, IV
    B. I, III, VI
    C. III, V
    D. V only

22. Which of the following is the CORRECT declaration of Boolean type?
    A. boolean b1 = 0;
    B. boolean b2 = 'false';
    C. boolean b3 = false;
    D. boolean b4 = Boolean.false();
    E. boolean b5 = no;

23.
```
class Equals
{
public static void main (String[]args)
{
int x = 700;
double y = 700.1;
boolean b = (x=y);
System.out,println(b);
}
}
```
What will be the output of the above program?
    A. True
    B. False
    C. compilation error
    D. An exception at runtime

24.
```
public class Test
{
public static void leftshift(int i , int j)
{
i<<=j;
}
public static void main(String args[])
{
int i = 4, j = 2;
leftshift(i,j);
System.out.println(i);
}
}
```
What will be the output of the above program?
    A. 2
    B. 4
    C. 8
    D. 16

25.
```
class Test
{
static int s;
public static void main(String[]args)
{
Test product = new Test ();
product.start();
System.out,println(s);
}

void start()
{
int x = 7;
twice(x);
System.out.print(x+" ");
}

void twice(int x)
{
x = x*2;
s = x;
}
}
```
What will be the output of the above program?
  A. 7 7   B. 7 14   C. 14 0   D. 14 14

KEY (CORRECT ANSWERS)

1. D
2. A
3. A
4. A
5. D

6. A
7. B
8. A
9. B
10. C

11. D
12. B
13. B
14. D
15. C

16. C
17. C
18. D
19. C
20. B

21. B
22. C
23. C
24. B
25. B

TEST 3

DIRECTIONS: Each question or incomplete statement is followed by several suggested answers or completions. Select the one that BEST answers the question or completes the statement. *PRINT THE LETTER OF THE CORRECT ANSWER IN THE SPACE AT THE RIGHT.*

1. Which of the following is the core function of a record keeper? 1.____
   A. Classifying   B. Storing   C. Destroying
   D. All of the above   E. A and B only

2. Which of the following organizational data is a record? 2.____
   A. E-mail   B. Database data
   C. Non-business transactions   D. All of the above
   E. A and B only

3. _____ is a way to track the integrity of secured records. 3.____
   A. Access control   B. Security model
   C. Audit trail   D. Physical controls

4. _____ is NOT relevant for the preservation of records. 4.____
   A. Period of retention   B. Internal policy
   C. Media   D. Physical checks

5. Which of the following is not a command found within an Excel spreadsheet? 5.____
   A. Print   B. OCR
   C. Formula   D. Sort

6. To create a formula in an Excel sheet, the user should look for which of the following symbols? 6.____
   A. @   B. $ C. ^   D. *fx*

7. Data is arranged in rows and columns with column titles as headings. Which Excel function would you use to search data in one of the columns based on values sorted by the first column? 7.____
   A. Find()   B. Vlookup()   C. Search()   D. Locate()

8. An operator would generate pivot tables for 8.____
   A. automatically producing summary data
   B. making search faster
   C. working with data at multiple spreadsheets
   D. reusing same data at other locations

9. Your spreadsheet data has grown beyond the maximum rows, causing your searches to slow down and the spreadsheet file taking long to open. Which of the following is a solution to this problem?
   A. Export data to multiple spreadsheets
   B. Switch to database solution
   C. Archive data and start afresh
   D. Delete some records

10. Which of the following field types would be used to store images of documents in a database record?
    A. Boolean   B. Memo   C. Variant   D. BLOB

11. Which one of the following is a document management system?
    A. Outlook   B. Sharepoint
    C. Google calendar   D. Ical
    E. All of the above

12. CRM stands for
    A. Creative Record Management
    B. Creative Resource Management
    C. Customer Relationship Management
    D. Customer Resource Manipulation

13. _____ is a standard for integrating into corporate cloud sources.
    A. REST   B. OData   C. A and B   D. A only

14.

	A	B	C
1	Days	Amount Spent	Running
2	Day 1	$20	
3	Day 2	$56	
4	Day 3	$78	
5	Day 4	$89	
6	Day 5	$90	
7	Day 6	$104	
8	Day 7	$301	

Consider the above spreadsheet snapshot.
Which of the following is the correct formula for calculating running totals that can be copied to the rest of the column?
   A. =sum(C2:c2)   B. -sum(c$2:c2)
   C. =sum($C$2:c2)   D. =sum($c2:c2)

15. In the previous question, we now need to count the occurrences of "Day 1". 15.____
    Which option below could be a way of doing this?
    A. =IF(a2="Day 1",COUNTIF($B$2:B8,B2),"")
    B. IF(a2="Day 1",COUNTIF(B8:B2),"")
    C. IF(a2="Day 1",COUNT(B8:B2),"")
    D. IF(a2="Day 1",COUNT(!B2),"")

16. Your organization wants to check the balance of its assets and liabilities. 16.____
    Which of the following statements would you generate?
    A. Balance sheet   B. Trial balance
    C. Cash flow   D. Journal

17. An e-mail needs to be distributed to contacts in different departments, though 17.____
    the recipients should not see who else received the e-mail? The e-mail should be
    sent using
    A. BCC   B. CC   C. Outlook   D. hide function

18. A company has long backed up documents, spreadsheets and other office files 18.____
    on rewritable CDs but is now looking for a storage solution with higher capacity and
    less physical space. Which of the following would NOT solve the problem?
    A. Cloud-based storage   B. External hard drives
    C. Flash drives   D. Upgraded operating system

19. Record lifecycle and system lifecycle 19.____
    A. are the same disciplines
    B. must be applied separately
    C. depend on manual or electronic ways of storage
    D. system lifecycle has a broader scope

20. Changes in company revenue over time is best displayed as a _____ graph. 20.____
    A. line   B. bar   C. pie   D. bubble

21. A formula correctly written to add a column of inventory figures should begin with 21.____
    A. +=TOTAL   B. =ADD
    C. =SUM   D. =TOTAL

22. Your supervisor requests that department e-mails be classified so they are 22.____
    easier to find and retrieve. The BEST way to accomplish this would be to
    A. create category folders
    B. strengthen the junk-mail filter
    C. create alternate e-mail addresses
    D. flag all pertinent e-mails as important/urgent

23. Appraisal is the 23.____
    A. record cleaning for keeping only the required data
    B. process of deciding if a record is to be kept or destroyed
    C. safe custody of information
    D. analysis of the storage medium used for safekeeping

24. A list of types of records and the period for keeping them before permanently destroying is called
    A. recording memo
    B. retention schedule
    C. record profile
    D. archive summary

25. _____ is a structure used for material classification into groups and subgroups.
    A. Taxonomy
    B. Virology
    C. Synonymy
    D. Axiology

KEY (CORRECT ANSWERS)

1.	D		11.	B
2.	D		12.	B
3.	C		13.	C
4.	B		14.	C
5.	B		15.	A
6.	D		16.	A
7.	B		17.	A
8.	A		18.	D
9.	B		19.	B
10.	D		20.	A

21. C
22. A
23. B
24. B
25. A

TEST 4

DIRECTIONS: Each question or incomplete statement is followed by several suggested answers or completions. Select the one that BEST answers the question or completes the statement. *PRINT THE LETTER OF THE CORRECT ANSWER IN THE SPACE AT THE RIGHT.*

1. At the front desk you are answering a client call. A fax arrives, a courier jumps in with a parcel to be received and multiple phones start ringing. Which one of the following would be the BEST possible way to handle the situation?   1.____
    A. Handle all the transactions one by one in random order one at a time
    B. All calls first, courier to follow, and then the fax
    C. A smile to the courier, put all other lines on hold, finish with the present call, and look at the fax and receive the parcel
    D. Hand over the fax to the courier for reading and attend to the present call and put all other calls on hold

2. A user says his computer takes a very long time to start up, and that he often must wait 5-10 minutes before he is able to conduct basic operations on his PC like opening a document or Internet browser. The most likely reason for this delay is   2.____
    A. a damaged router
    B. slow network connection
    C. an outdated web browser
    D. too many programs running at startup

3. Assume you work for a call center supporting a renowned software company. Without warning, the usual support staff is temporarily unavailable. Which support step would be MOST important?   3.____
    A. Supervisors change roles and work as operators
    B. Operators work multiple shifts
    C. Automated answering is doubled
    D. Prioritizing of important tasks and following the order

4. You disagree with a client's aggressive opinion about a faulty product feature. Which of the following would be appropriate?   4.____
    A. Tell the client you'll reply once you've discussed the issue with a supervisor
    B. Let the client know you understand and follow with troubleshooting
    C. Let the client know you understand but politely refuse
    D. Escalate the issue for the next tier of support

5. A customer reports being frustrated with numerous attempts to resolve her problem.
   What is the FIRST thing that you should do?
   A. Tell the customer that you understand her problem
   B. Avoid conflict
   C. Confront the problem and not the customer
   D. Listen to the customer without making any comments

6. How do you handle and support a non-native chat using a messaging tool in a foreign language?
   A. Use sign language
   B. Make use of a translation tool
   C. Avoid contact
   D. Such a situation is not for you to handle

7. Which of the following is the BEST way to handle a customer call when you do not know the correct solution to a problem?
   A. Try to give a best possible answer
   B. Tell her the problem could be user error
   C. Delay the query until you have a solution
   D. Tell her that you do not know the answer and you will consult a supervisor

8. A client's computer time again leaves the network.
   Which one of the following is the MOST possible reason?
   A. DLL
   B. NIC driver
   C. VPN configuration
   D. Operating system

9. Which of the following should be used to install MS Windows on multiple systems on the same network?
   A. EaseUS Todo Backup
   B. System image
   C. Hosting server
   D. A and B above

10. Which of the following solutions might solve basic issues in the operating system?
    A. Restart system
    B. Update operating system/application
    C. Diagnostics tool
    D. Check hardware

11. A research organization approaches the help desk for testing the software application in their recommended environment.
    What level of support would handle the request?
    A. L1
    B. L2
    C. L3
    D. L4

3 (#4)

12. Clients are able to resolve most of their problems by reading the FAQs provided on the product support site or watching troubleshooting videos. The user queries are MOSTLY handled on
    A. T0 and T1   B. T1 only   C. T2   D. T3

12.____

13. To support less technical users, a technician may connect to a user computer via the internet. This is called
    A. Level 0 support
    B. TCP/IP support
    C. Remote computer repair
    D. Modular repair support

13.____

14. The service provider is billing the company for work done on an actual basis. Which of the following is the mode of support?
    A. Managed services
    B. Break/Fix
    C. On-demand outsourcing
    D. Cloud servicing

14.____

15. The term SMB is used for
    A. Small Businesses
    B. Small Marginal Brokerage
    C. Similar Main Brokerage
    D. Small and Medium-Sized Businesses

15.____

16. Which of the following is a type of technical support where the end users interact with each other using discussion boards to solve each other's issues?
    A. Managed services
    B. Block hours
    C. Call in
    D. Crowdsourced technical support

16.____

17. Being a member of Level 1 support team, you would ideally resolve _____ percent of the queries/support issues.
    A. 50   B. 60   C. 70   D. 80

17.____

18. Password issues would generally be resolved by a call center called
    A. front-end support
    B. initial sink
    C. back-end team
    D. CRUD

18.____

19. Hardware-related issues are normally escalated to
    A. L2   B. L3   C. L4   D. L0

19.____

20. Customer support specialists may provide services from anywhere around the world. They operate from call centers in possibly remote countries. They are referred to as
    A. ISP   B. MSP   C. JSP   D. SSP

20.____

21. A customer reports a stolen credit card. As a call center representative, you provide best details to the team responsible for blocking any misuse. This escalation and data reporting takes place at tier
    A. T1   B. T3   C. T4   D. T0

21.____

22. Which one of the following is possibly handled at an escalation point beyond the organization representing the supported software product?
    A. Application failure
    B. Validation of login credentials
    C. Addition of a critical feature
    D. Reporting a warning message

23. Which one of the following will allow first-level support only?
    A. ISP   B. Banks   C. Industries   D. Army

24. A help desk organization may sign a service agreement with a service provider for _____ services.
    A. managed   B. primitive   C. dedicated   D. multilayered

25. Which of the following ISO standards applies to information security in the cloud for a service desk?
    A. ISO 2984   B. ISO 27001   C. ISO 2008   D. ISO 1001

KEY (CORRECT ANSWERS)

1.	C		11.	D
2.	D		12.	A
3.	D		13.	C
4.	A		14.	C
5.	A		15.	D
6.	B		16.	D
7.	D		17.	D
8.	B		18.	B
9.	D		19.	A
10.	A		20.	B

21.	A
22.	C
23.	A
24.	A
25.	B

EXAMINATION SECTION
TEST 1

DIRECTIONS: Each question or incomplete statement is followed by several suggested answers or completions. Select the one that BEST answers the question or completes the statement. *PRINT THE LETTER OF THE CORRECT ANSWER IN THE SPACE AT THE RIGHT.*

1. When deciding the means by which training is to be delivered, the designer of instruction should FIRST select the
    A. type of delivery system technology
    B. trainer
    C. necessary instructional properties
    D. delivery system

    1.____

2. _____ does NOT directly involve instruction, but offers the power to make learning more efficient.
    A. Computer-managed instruction (CMI)
    B. Computer-based training (CBT)
    C. Technical training function (TTF)
    D. Computer-assisted instruction (CAI)

    2.____

3. The use of case studies as a means of instructional delivery should be avoided when
    A. training involves management or supervisory personnel
    B. instructional goals include critical thinking
    C. there is unhealthy competition among trainees
    D. time constraints on preparation exist

    3.____

4. Each of the following is a function of audience response systems (ARS) software EXCEPT
    A. analyzing group responses to items
    B. performing demographic analyses
    C. storing scores for later analysis
    D. administering progressive evaluations during instruction

    4.____

5. Which of the following is a step typically involved in the design phase of instructional design?
    A. Pilot instruction
    B. Developing instructional materials
    C. Analyzing job tasks
    D. Developing testing strategies

    5.____

6. Which of the following is NOT a typical component of a performance support system (PSS)?
    A. Expert system
    B. Printed job aids
    C. Text retrieval
    D. Computer-aided instruction

    6.____

7. An expert system includes knowledge structured for capturing regularly occurring circumstances. This structured knowledge is known as

   A. logic
   B. frames
   C. neural network processing
   D. rules

8. In a training situation, a(n) _____ is MOST likely to be held liable for misrepresentation.

   A. employer
   B. outside contractors/vendors
   C. owner/employer
   D. trainer

9. A good computer-assisted instruction delivery system will use

   A. norming
   B. scrolling
   C. page-turning
   D. branching

10. Each of the following is usually considered to be a characteristic of effective instructional design EXCEPT

    A. rule-based design
    B. holistic self-evaluation
    C. interconnected tasks
    D. systematic approach

11. Instructional media are typically used to

    A. direct learning activities
    B. predict the best method of instructional delivery
    C. support learning activities
    D. evaluate trainee performance

12. Which of the following instructional delivery techniques typically involves the LOWEST development cost?

    A. Audiotape
    B. Multimedia computer
    C. Lecture
    D. Live video

13. Computer-aided instruction is often designed so that only the precise knowledge needed at that point in the activity is taught.
    This is referred to as _____ CAI.

    A. secular
    B. granular
    C. partitioned
    D. modular

14. Each of the following is an advantage associated with the use of vendors as trainers EXCEPT

    A. no additional strain on training budget
    B. initiation of function that can later be turned over to in-house trainer
    C. usual offering of continued support
    D. proficiency in using new equipment or machines

15. Which of the following is a mode of computer-supported learning resources?

    A. Evaluation
    B. Tutorial
    C. Instructional games
    D. Hypermedia

16. Which of the following conditions does NOT typically indicate the use of performance support devices?

    A. Regulation requirements
    B. Frequently changing tasks
    C. Infrequently performed tasks
    D. Cost of mistakes is relatively low

17. Which of the following performance support devices can MOST accurately be described as *procedural*?

    A. Printed job aids
    B. Computer-based references (CBR)
    C. Hypertext
    D. Computer help systems

18. If a typical instructor-led training delivery system requires ten hours of instructional time, a textual computer-based training approach will typically require about _____ instructional hours.

    A. 40   B. 100   C. 200   D. 400

19. Which of the following is an advantage associated with the use of performance observation as a means of gathering data during instructional design?

    A. Immediate response availability
    B. Minimal disturbance in work routines
    C. Generation of motivational information
    D. Low relative cost

20. Each of the following is a mode of computer-managed instruction EXCEPT

    A. record keeping
    B. simulation
    C. prescription generation
    D. testing

21. Which of the following is typically addressed in the evaluation strategy produced during instructional design?

    A. Balance of activities encompassed by the design
    B. Development of instructional materials
    C. Outcomes required to satisfy each performance criterion
    D. Provision of learner reinforcement

22. As a means of instructional delivery, role playing is useful under each of the following conditions EXCEPT when

    A. training involves the application of content knowledge
    B. technical or psychomotor skills are the focus
    C. training involves management or supervisory personnel
    D. instructional objectives are concerned with interpersonal relations

23. _____ is NOT a step typically involved in the analysis phase of instructional design.

    A. Writing instructional objectives
    B. Selecting tasks for training
    C. Determining instructional prerequisites
    D. Assessing learning requirements

24. Instruction delivered to new employees before they begin regular work is called _____ training.

    A. OJT   B. vestibule
    C. independent study   D. apprenticeship

25. If a company decides to contract out to an external training provider, each of the following elements must be included in a request for proposal EXCEPT

    A. project background   B. outputs and deliverables
    C. delivery strategy   D. project procedures

KEY (CORRECT ANSWERS)

1. C		11. C
2. A		12. C
3. D		13. B
4. D		14. B
5. D		15. D
6. B		16. D
7. B		17. A
8. B		18. C
9. D		19. B
10. B		20. B

21. C
22. B
23. C
24. B
25. C

TEST 2

DIRECTIONS: Each question or incomplete statement is followed by several suggested answers or completions. Select the one that BEST answers the question or completes the statement. *PRINT THE LETTER OF THE CORRECT ANSWER IN THE SPACE AT THE RIGHT.*

1. It is a good idea to use lecturing as a method of instructional delivery when 1.____

    A. complex processes need to be explained
    B. introducing training provided by other methods or media
    C. the trainer is unfamiliar with the audience
    D. instructional goals deal with affective or psycho-motor skills

2. Typically, the LARGEST part of all training costs is 2.____

    A. job aids
    B. vendor contracts
    C. travel expense associated with off-site training
    D. trainee salary during training

3. The systemic approach to training evaluation is typically divided into four parts. Which of the following is NOT one of these parts? 3.____

    A. Identification of trainee prerequisites
    B. Identification of training goals
    C. Production of learning outcomes
    D. Support performance development

4. During the instructional design process, an analysis document is produced which includes specifications for each of the following EXCEPT 4.____

    A. measurement factors
    B. target audience characteristics
    C. instructional media
    D. program management

5. Each of the following is a disadvantage associated with the use of employee-trainers EXCEPT 5.____

    A. least economical for recurrent training needs
    B. increased head count in labor budget
    C. less likely to have knowledge of adult learning techniques
    D. lack of knowledge of new-hire trainers

6. Which of the following is NOT among the modes of computer-assisted instruction? 6.____

    A. Problem solving   B. Calculation
    C. Modeling   D. Drill and practice

7. Which of the following performance support devices offers the GREATEST availability to trainees? 7.____

    A. Printed job aids   B. Expert systems
    C. Hypertext   D. Computer help systems

83

8. Demonstrations might be used as a method of instructional delivery when

   A. instructional goals involve cognitive or affective domains
   B. dealing with especially large groups of trainees
   C. tasks require manual dexterity or are difficult for learners to understand
   D. when materials and equipment are scarce

9. Which of the following is typically addressed during the implementation phase of instructional design?

   A. Revision of instructional materials
   B. Selection of tasks for training
   C. Creation of design syllabus
   D. Creation of delivery strategy

10. The psychomotor domain of learning progresses in four discrete stages. Which of the following stages is typically the LAST to be accomplished?

    A. Manipulation   B. Articulation
    C. Imitation   D. Precision

11. A well-written instructional objective should include three key components. Which of the following is NOT one of these?

    A. Conditions   B. Performance
    C. Media   D. Criteria

12. If a job requires high technical knowledge but low manual skill, which of the following learning methods would be BEST suited for job training?

    A. Self-study and lab
    B. Classroom and on-the-job training with mentor
    C. Classroom and lab
    D. Classroom and self-practice

13. The computer- _____ component of technology-based training does NOT actually teach or manage instruction, but serves to make learning easier and more appropriate.

    A. managed instruction (CMI)
    B. based training (CBT)
    C. supported learning resource (CSLR)
    D. assisted instruction (CAI)

14. _____ simulation is used in information systems training.

    A. Manual   B. Hybrid
    C. Sequential   D. Computer

15. In order for trainees to move nonsequentially through a computerized training document, _____ will need to be installed.

    A. an expert system   B. hypertext
    C. an authoring system   D. a hierarchy

16. If a job requires high technical knowledge and manual skill, which of the following learning methods would be BEST suited for job training?

    A. Self-study and lab
    B. Classroom and on-the-job training with mentor
    C. Classroom and lab
    D. Classroom and self-practice

17. Which of the following is typically addressed in the design syllabus created during instructional design?

    A. Sequence in which content is presented
    B. Evaluation of training objectives
    C. Means of administering precourse assessment
    D. Evaluation of prerequisite skills

18. The use of peer tutoring as a method of instructional delivery will usually have all of the following benefits EXCEPT

    A. facilitating pacing of instruction in groups with heterogeneous abilities
    B. encouraging competition among trainees
    C. easing trainer"s workload
    D. increasing trainee's satisfaction with instruction

19. Which of the following instructional delivery techniques typically offers the GREATEST opportunity for self-pacing?

    A. Audiotape   B. Multimedia computer
    C. Lecture   D. Live video

20. In the development of technology-based training, the logical starting point is computer-

    A. managed instruction (CMI)
    B. based training (CBT)
    C. supported learning resources (CSLR)
    D. assisted instruction (CAI)

21. As a means of instructional delivery, case studies are MOST useful for

    A. very large groups of trainees
    B. bridging theory and practice
    C. shaping attitudinal objectives
    D. drill and practice of psychomotor skills

22. An advantage commonly associated with the use of consultants as trainers is

    A. employees may be able to earn college credit for training course
    B. no increase in labor budget
    C. availability for modular training
    D. *one-shot* training

23. Discussion should be avoided as a method of instructional delivery when

    A. dealing with a group of trainees that is forty or larger
    B. content is rigid and restricted to facts
    C. there are strict time constraints on instruction
    D. instructional goals deal with attitudes or critical thinking skills

24. The component of technology-based learning that actually teaches is

    A. computer-managed instruction (CMI)
    B. computer-based training (CBT)
    C. technical training function (TTF)
    D. computer-assisted instruction (CAI)

25. Which of the following instructional delivery approaches would typically require the FEWEST number of development hours?

    A. Textual computer-based training
    B. Workbook
    C. Videotape
    D. Instructor-led

KEY (CORRECT ANSWERS)

1.	B	11.	C
2.	D	12.	D
3.	A	13.	C
4.	C	14.	D
5.	A	15.	B
6.	B	16.	B
7.	A	17.	A
8.	C	18.	B
9.	A	19.	B
10.	B	20.	A

21.	B
22.	B
23.	C
24.	D
25.	D

EXAMINATION SECTION

TEST 1

DIRECTIONS: Each question or incomplete statement is followed by several suggested answers or completions. Select the one that BEST answers the question or completes the statement. *PRINT THE LETTER OF THE CORRECT ANSWER IN THE SPACE AT THE RIGHT.*

1. The primary storage is
   - A. used by processor
   - B. used by RAM
   - C. both A and B
   - D. none of the above

2. Clock speed is measured in
   - A. hertz
   - B. megahertz
   - C. gigahertz
   - D. none of the above

3. Which of the following temperatures can cause component failure?
   - A. 180 degrees
   - B. 185 degrees
   - C. 190 degrees
   - D. 205 degrees

4. A motherboard has _____ connections to the power supply.
   - A. one or more
   - B. just one
   - C. two
   - D. none of the above

5. CMOS setup is used
   - A. to change motherboard settings
   - B. for basic input/output
   - C. both A and B
   - D. none of the above

6. ROM chips that can be overwritten are known as
   - A. flash ROM
   - B. micro ROM
   - C. BIOS
   - D. none of the above

7. A secure way of transferring files from one device to another is
   - A. FTP
   - B. TFTP
   - C. SFTP
   - D. none of the above

8. A method to provide access to a VPN is
   - A. RAS
   - B. PPP
   - C. PPTP
   - D. IGP

9. A big advantage of having a wireless standard is
   - A. interoperability between devices
   - B. greater device security
   - C. both A and B
   - D. none of the above

10. When you are implementing a basic wireless network,
    - A. disable ESSID broadcast
    - B. don't configure the ESSID point
    - C. both A and B
    - D. none of the above

11. You are installing a device that can throttle and detect peer-to-peer traffic. This device belongs to the device type
    A. load balancer
    B. bandwidth shaper
    C. proxy server
    D. none of the above

12. The first step involved in troubleshooting after arriving on the site is
    A. identifying the symptoms and drawing a network diagram
    B. comparing wiring schematics to the industry standards
    C. both A and B
    D. none of the above

13. _____ describes an email that has web links to direct users to malicious websites.
    A. Phishing
    B. Viruses
    C. Both A and B
    D. None of the above

14. You are troubleshooting network connectivity and want to see the path that the packets are taking from a workstation to the server. The _____ command line tool will be used for this.
    A. ping
    B. traceroute
    C. route
    D. nslookup

15. The process or steps required to be applied to develop an information system is
    A. system development life cycle
    B. program specification
    C. design cycle
    D. analytical code

16. Project plan is a document
    A. describing how the project team will develop the proposed system
    B. that outlines the technical feasibility of the proposed system
    C. both A and B
    D. none of the above

17. The primary goal of a system analyst is to
    A. create value for the organization
    B. create a wonderful system
    C. acquire a working tool
    D. none of the above

18. Understanding the purpose of the information system to be built and finding out how the project team is to accomplish making it is part of the _____ phase of the SDLC.
    A. analysis
    B. system request
    C. planning
    D. none of the above

19. Examining the economic, technical and organizational advantages and disadvantages of developing a new system is known as
    A. feasibility analysis
    B. committee approval
    C. risk analysis
    D. system request

20. The calculation measuring the amount of money an organization is going to get in return for the money it has spent is known as
    A. cash flow
    B. return on investment
    C. tangible costs
    D. none of the above

21. New users should be encouraged to use software by taking help first from
    A. tutorial software
    B. training software
    C. both A and B
    D. none of the above

22. A wizard is
    A. a person who can do magic
    B. software that helps and walks user through a complex process
    C. hardware that speeds up performance
    D. all of the above

23. How can you determine the level of a trainee's knowledge?
    A. By watching them type
    B. By taking a test
    C. By asking them questions
    D. Both B and C

24. Which of the following is the most important step when giving training users?
    A. Make them want to learn
    B. Push them until they master the task
    C. Leave learning or not learning up to them; just provide the training
    D. None of the above

25. It is important that while training, the trainees are shown the
    A. training agenda
    B. results of previous training sessions
    C. trainer's achievements
    D. none of the above

KEY (CORRECT ANSWERS)

1. C
2. A
3. B
4. A
5. A

6. A
7. C
8. C
9. A
10. A

11. B
12. A
13. A
14. B
15. A

16. A
17. A
18. C
19. A
20. B

21. C
22. B
23. C
24. A
25. A

___

TEST 2

DIRECTIONS: Each question or incomplete statement is followed by several suggested answers or completions. Select the one that BEST answers the question or completes the statement. *PRINT THE LETTER OF THE CORRECT ANSWER IN THE SPACE AT THE RIGHT.*

1. _____ makes it possible for the system to power up with the help of a keyboard.
   A. ACPI
   B. APM
   C. Both A and B
   D. None of the above

   1.____

2. Which of the following are data path sizes?
   A. 8, 16
   B. 32, 64
   C. 128
   D. All of the above

   2.____

3. The lines that carry the data in a bus is known as
   A. data bus
   B. memory bus
   C. micro bus
   D. none of the above

   3.____

4. Which of the following can be used to boot, recover or reinstall the Windows operating system?
   A. Recovery CD
   B. Windows CD
   C. Memory CD
   D. None of the above

   4.____

5. Which of the following explains the proper handling of substances like chemical solvents?
   A. Material safety data sheet
   B. POST
   C. Memory data sheet
   D. None of the above

   5.____

6. A _____ tests a USB, networks, serial or other port.
   A. loop back plug
   B. three-head plug
   C. both A and B
   D. none of the above

   6.____

7. Bundling network cables can cause
   A. crosstalk
   B. attenuation
   C. collision
   D. none of the above

   7.____

8. The greatest concern while using an orbital satellite WAN link is
   A. cable length
   B. duplex
   C. latency
   D. collision

   8.____

9. If packets to an IP address are dropping over the Internet, _____ will be used to determine the responsible hop.
   A. netstat
   B. traceroute
   C. ping
   D. none of the above

   9.____

10. _____ ports can be used for FTP traffic.
    A. 25
    B. 24
    C. 23
    D. 20

    10.____

11. The _____ connects multiple workstations, functions as a router and supports VLANs.
    A. hub
    B. multilayer switch
    C. switch
    D. repeater

12. To provide VoIP phones with power but without having to arrange independent power supplies for them, the switches on the network should have
    A. spanning tree
    B. PoE
    C. PPPoE
    D. VLAN tagging

13. _____ has the same functionality as Telnet but operates more securely.
    A. SSH
    B. RSH
    C. TFTP
    D. SNAT

14. You use a logical network diagram to determine the number of
    A. cables in the network
    B. broadcast domains on the network
    C. users on the network
    D. none of the above

15. Planning and controlling the system development within a deadline at the lowest cost and with the right functionality is called
    A. project management
    B. task identification
    C. task
    D. none of the above

16. One way of calculating project completion time is to apply industry standard factors for each phase of the project. In this method, the planning phase takes almost 15% of the total time. If a project takes three months for planning, then the remaining project will need approximately
    A. 20 months
    B. 15 months
    C. 3 months
    D. none of the above

17. Fourteen factors impact the complexity of a project when we are using a function point estimation worksheet. _____ are included in these factors.
    A. Data communications, end user efficiency and reusability
    B. Data communications, estimated effort and time tradeoffs
    C. Both A and B
    D. None of the above

18. In determining the tasks for a work plan, you can
    A. list the four phases of SDLC and steps occurring in each phase
    B. control and direct the project
    C. establish a possible reporting structure
    D. none of the above

19. If someone is examining existing paperwork so that he can better understand the As-Is system, this is
    A. observation
    B. JAD
    C. document analysis
    D. none of the above

3 (#2)

20. _____ is an information-gathering technique that helps an analyst to find out facts and opinions from a large number of geographically dispersed people.
    A. Questionnaire
    B. Document analysis
    C. JAD session
    D. None of the above

20.____

21. All of the following are examples of privacy and security risks EXCEPT
    A. viruses
    B. spam
    C. hackers
    D. Trojan horses

21.____

22. _____ can recover a deleted/damaged file of a computer.
    A. Robotics
    B. Simulation
    C. Both A and B
    D. None of the above

22.____

23. _____ language is used by the computer to process data.
    A. Binary
    B. Processing
    C. Both A and B
    D. None of the above

23.____

24. The operating system
    A. enables drawing of a flowchart
    B. provides user-friendly interface
    C. both A and B
    D. none of the above

24.____

25. _____ is not an application software package.
    A. Microsoft Office
    B. Redhat Linux
    C. Adobe PageMaker
    D. Microsoft PowerPoint

25.____

KEY (CORRECT ANSWERS)

1.	A		11.	B
2.	D		12.	B
3.	A		13.	A
4.	A		14.	B
5.	A		15.	A
6.	A		16.	A
7.	A		17.	A
8.	C		18.	A
9.	B		19.	C
10.	D		20.	A

21. B
22. D
23. A
24. B
25. B

TEST 3

DIRECTIONS: Each question or incomplete statement is followed by several suggested answers or completions. Select the one that BEST answers the question or completes the statement. *PRINT THE LETTER OF THE CORRECT ANSWER IN THE SPACE AT THE RIGHT.*

1. The character repeat rate can be adjusted in
   A. Control Panel > Keyboard
   B. My Computer
   C. Recycle Bin
   D. none of the above

   1.____

2. There are _____ means of using a wireless mouse.
   A. 1
   B. 2
   C. 3
   D. none of the above

   2.____

3. _____ is used for creating and manipulating sound.
   A. MIDI
   B. SIDI
   C. MODO
   D. None of the above

   3.____

4. Picture quality is expressed in
   A. megapixels
   B. hexapixels
   C. both of the above
   D. none of the above

   4.____

5. The microphone port is located on the
   A. sound card
   B. motherboard
   C. driver
   D. none of the above

   5.____

6. The _____ is the peripheral device that transfers the audio from the PC.
   A. headphones
   B. microphone
   C. camera
   D. all of the above

   6.____

7. _____ is a secure connection.
   A. HTTP   B. TELNET   C. HTTPs   D. RCP

   7.____

8. A computer can be a client and a server to other computers in a _____ network.
   A. bus   B. VPN   C. ring   D. peer-to-peer

   8.____

9. A _____ is used to send a signal at one end of a cable and found at the other end of the cable.
   A. cable tester
   B. toner probe
   C. multimeter
   D. none of the above

   9.____

10. A company's ISP uses _____ to troubleshoot network issues.
    A. Smart Jack   B. 110 Block   C. 66 Block   D. Demarc

    10.____

11. A firewall has not blocked a remote web server. To verify this, a _____ can be used.
    A. port scanner
    B. toner probe
    C. both A and B
    D. none of the above

12. _____ should be enabled to prevent broadcast storms.
    A. Bonding
    B. Spanning tree
    C. Port mirroring
    D. DHCP

13. A _____ network is least likely to collide.
    A. bus
    B. star
    C. ring
    D. mesh

14. _____ tests the operation of NIC.
    A. Crossover
    B. Rollover
    C. 568B
    D. Loopback

15. Planning includes
    A. conducting preliminary investigation
    B. conducting feasibility study
    C. identifying constraints
    D. all of the above

16. Feasibility study types include
    A. technical
    B. economic return
    C. non-economic return
    D. all of the above

17. Analysis includes
    A. gathering competent team members
    B. sending instructions to users
    C. documenting the existing system
    D. all of the above

18. The design phase includes determining
    A. technical systems configuration
    B. data structure
    C. make or buy decision
    D. all of the above

19. Which one of the following is a type of documentation?
    A. System documentation
    B. Document feeder
    C. Audio coding
    D. None of the above

20. The implementation phase includes
    A. conducting cutover
    B. training users
    C. managing change
    D. all of the above

21. Processing takes place at the
    A. box
    B. CPU
    C. system unit
    D. motherboard

22. Memory is of _____ type(s).
    A. one
    B. two
    C. three
    D. four

23. The _____ card is used while playing a video game.
    A. sound
    B. graphic
    C. modem
    D. network information

24. To do a specific task, a set of instructions is given to the computer. This most closely describes
    A. software
    B. hardware
    C. Internet browsing
    D. none of the above

25. A user is allowed to analyze and maintain a computer by a program called
    A. Utility
    B. Windows XP
    C. MS Office
    D. Device Driver

KEY (CORRECT ANSWERS)

1.	A	11.	A
2.	B	12.	B
3.	A	13.	C
4.	A	14.	D
5.	A	15.	D
6.	A	16.	D
7.	C	17.	C
8.	D	18.	D
9.	A	19.	A
10.	A	20.	D

21. C
22. B
23. A
24. A
25. A

TEST 4

DIRECTIONS: Each question or incomplete statement is followed by several suggested answers or completions. Select the one that BEST answers the question or completes the statement. *PRINT THE LETTER OF THE CORRECT ANSWER IN THE SPACE AT THE RIGHT.*

1. A(n) _____ is a device resembling a hypodermic needle. 1.____
   A. extractor
   B. detracter
   C. loop back plug
   D. none of the above

2. Which of the following are components of the microcomputer? 2.____
   A. Memory, Unit System
   B. Input device
   C. Output device
   D. All of the above

3. _____ is a common type of keyboard. 3.____
   A. USB
   B. PS/2
   C. Both A and B
   D. None of the above

4. How can we differentiate between a mouse's and keyboard's port? 4.____
   A. Keyboard is purple and mouse is green
   B. Keyboard is green and mouse is purple
   C. Keyboard is blue and mouse is green
   D. None of the above

5. If you reboot your computer and receive an error message of BIOS keyboard, 5.____
   A. the mouse is plugged into the keyboard input
   B. the keyboard is plugged into the mouse input
   C. both A and B
   D. none of the above

6. The mouse settings can be adjusted in 6.____
   A. Control Panel
   B. DOS
   C. My Computer
   D. none of the above

7. _____ prevents the propagating of different departments network broadcasts if they are located on the same switch. 7.____
   A. Hub   B. VLAN   C. Firewall   D. Trunk

8. The most secure protocol for transferring network device configuration is 8.____
   A. TFTP
   B. RCP
   C. SCP
   D. none of the above

9. _____ Internet devices operate the OSI layer. 9.____
   A. One   B. Two   C. Three   D. Four

10. You need to determine which buildings have multimode or single mode fiber. You will use the
    A. security policy
    B. physical network diagram
    C. baseline configuration
    D. none of the above

11. Many users are complaining about network issues. Of the following steps, which will you take FIRST?
    A. Collect information about the symptoms
    B. Make a plan of action and a solution
    C. Document the solution
    D. None of the above

12. Employees utilizing wireless laptops outdoors at the office are experiencing new connectivity problems. _____ is/are most likely causing the problems.
    A. Signal bounce
    B. Antenna distance
    C. Environment factors
    D. None of the above

13. The _____ contain(s) information about unlabeled data center connections.
    A. wiring schematics
    B. emergency call list
    C. procedures manual
    D. none of the above

14. If you have to install a phone that needs only one wire for both data and power to be supplied, _____ must be supported by the switch.
    A. PoE
    B. spanning tree
    C. VLAN
    D. none of the above

15. During the analysis phase, _____ is the type of prototype.
    A. discovery
    B. evolving
    C. functioning
    D. none of the above

16. _____ is a review technique that checks the validity of the documents produced during system analysis.
    A. Structured walkthrough
    B. Prototyping
    C. Joint application
    D. None of the above

17. Implementation classes
    A. describe the user interface
    B. show implementation rules
    C. describe database interactions
    D. none of the above

18. Databases and file definition are prepared in the _____ phase.
    A. implementation
    B. design
    C. analysis
    D. none of the above

19. _____ is requirements analysis deliverables.
    A. Requirement specification
    B. User manual
    C. Design specification
    D. All of the above

20. _____ can help an analyst to work with users to find out system usage. 20.____
    A. Use case B. Class
    C. Actor D. None of the above

21. _____ is a data-transfer technique. 21.____
    A. DMA B. CAD
    C. Both A and B D. None of the above

22. _____ devices are designed under electromechanical principle. 22.____
    A. Input B. Output
    C. Storage D. All of the above

23. A monitor consists of 23.____
    A. BRT B. ARU
    C. CRT D. none of the above

24. Exception is also known as 24.____
    A. interrupt B. traps
    C. system calls D. none of the above

25. _____ is a mutually exclusive operation. 25.____
    A. Signal instruction B. Wait instruction
    C. Both A and B D. None of the above

KEY (CORRECT ANSWERS)

1. A 11. A
2. D 12. C
3. C 13. A
4. A 14. A
5. C 15. A

6. A 16. A
7. B 17. A
8. C 18. A
9. C 19. A
10. B 20. A

21. A
22. A
23. C
24. C
25. C

EXAMINATION SECTION
TEST 1

DIRECTIONS: Each question or incomplete statement is followed by several suggested answers or completions. Select the one that BEST answers the question or completes the statement. *PRINT THE LETTER OF THE CORRECT ANSWER IN THE SPACE AT THE RIGHT.*

1. During troubleshooting, you want to see the number of connections which are open on the user machine. The _____ command will be used to see these connections.
    A. Arp
    B. Netstat
    C. NsLookup
    D. Netgear

2. Two users want their PCs to be connected for file sharing. A _____ cable would be used to connect their PCs.
    A. crossover
    B. loopback
    C. straight
    D. none of the above

3. A remote user complains that he is not able to connect to the office via VPN, though he has established Internet connectivity. What step should you take next to troubleshoot this situation?
    A. Find out if the user is using a valid VPN address and password
    B. Power cycle the VPN concentrator
    C. Reinstall the VPN client
    D. None of the above

4. A _____ server limits the availability of types of websites that LAN users have access to.
    A. DHCP
    B. DC
    C. proxy
    D. DNS

5. If you are asked by the head of the company to block certain websites for the employees, what should you configure on the workstation to do so?
    A. Port scanner
    B. Antivirus service
    C. Network-based firewall
    D. Host-based firewall

6. While troubleshooting a user's problems connecting to their network shares, you find out that the problem lies in the network cabling between the workstation and the switch. If all the other users are able to connect to the network, _____ will probably be the cause.
    A. crosstalk and interference occurring
    B. cable has been damaged or cut within the wall
    C. cable is not punched down properly at the punch panel
    D. none of the above

1.____
2.____
3.____
4.____
5.____
6.____

7. Users are reporting that on a Windows network they are not able to access any network resources. The users can ping the IP address and use it to connect to the network resources. The cause of the problem may be
   A. the file server is offline
   B. the DNS server is not resolving properly
   C. the domain controller is not responding
   D. none of the above

7.____

8. If you have to give access to 64 servers on a network, which subnet of the following will provide the required access while conserving the IP address?
   A. 192.168.1.0.23
   B. 192.168.1.0.24
   C. 192.168.1.0.25
   D. 192.168.1.0.26

8.____

9. You are called by a user due to connection issues. You should start troubleshooting by
   A. resetting the router
   B. installing a new NIC
   C. reinstalling the OS
   D. checking the LEDs on NIC

9.____

10. You are called to extend the data circuit to the other side of the office. _____ would be set up at the new location.
    A. ESD
    B. IDF
    C. MDF
    D. EMI

10.____

11. If a connection is punched down and noise is coming across the cable, which of the following tools would be used to identify the problem?
    A. Protocol analyzer
    B. Cable tester
    C. Multimeter
    D. None of the above

11.____

12. You have tested a cable and determined that it can successfully receive and send signals. A _____ can be used to determine the speed and condition of the signal.
    A. TDR
    B. toner probe
    C. voltage event recorder
    D. protocol analyzer

12.____

13. A network has many network printers with server-hosted queues. A client reports that they are not printing. It is verified that all tasks sent from the users' computers to the network printers fail. What should be your next step to troubleshoot this situation?
    A. Replace the printer
    B. Reboot the print server
    C. Power cycle the switch
    D. Try the printer from another PC

13.____

14. A visitor is insisting that he wants to use the company's wireless network on his laptop. DHCP is configured perfectly and a temporary WEP key is assigned to him, but his laptop is still not able to connect to the network because
    A. MAC filtering is enabled of the WAP
    B. the network is out of wireless connections
    C. the DNS server is not working properly
    D. none of the above

14.____

15. An accounting department employee's workstation needs to be connected to the accounting server but is only able to connect to the Internet. The _____ setting should be verified in this case.
   A. VPN
   B. WINS
   C. DNS
   D. VLAN

16. If you discover that the phone company has not installed the smart jack in the right location and it needs to be moved 23 meters to the computer room, a _____ should be requested.
   A. demark extension
   B. 66 block extension
   C. replacement smart jack
   D. none of the above

17. Remote users complain of not being able to access files from the file server. You should first check the
   A. connectivity
   B. access rights
   C. network resources
   D. user accounts

18. You can successfully remote into the company's server but you cannot connect to any other server's directories from the server itself; however, you can ping them via the IP address. What is the problem?
   A. DHCP is not properly configured
   B. DNS is not properly configured
   C. Server is on a different VLAN
   D. None of the above

19. A _____ will be used to relocate a T1 nearer to the switch for connectivity.
   A. patch panel
   B. smart jack
   C. 25 pair cable
   D. none of the above

20. Your organization has 2,500 users, and they have exhausted their Internet bandwidth. You discover that 96% of the traffic is comprised of web browsing. A _____ network device will be added to reduce the amount of Internet bandwidth.
   A. proxy server
   B. load balancer
   C. content switch
   D. none of the above

21. Which document will you reference to discover a rogue WAP?
   A. Policies
   B. Baseline
   C. Wiring schematics
   D. None of the above

22. _____ can allow you to restrict communication between network devices.
   A. ACL
   B. CIDR
   C. NAT
   D. DHCP

23. Your company has a number of traveling sales employees who need secure access to the company's resources from no trusted devices. A _____ VPN solution will be the MOST appropriate for this.
   A. L2TP
   B. IPSec
   C. PPTP
   D. SSL

24. You are troubleshooting a switch and have determined the symptoms. 24.____
What should you do next?
   A. Implement and test solution   B. Find out the scope of the problem
   C. Escalate the issue   D. None of the above

25. In order to find out a physical interface problem, which of the following cables 25.____
would you use?
   A. Loopback   B. Console   C. Rollover   D. Serial

KEY (CORRECT ANSWERS)

1. B
2. A
3. A
4. C
5. D

6. A
7. B
8. C
9. D
10. B

11. B
12. A
13. D
14. A
15. D

16. A
17. A
18. B
19. B
20. A

21. B
22. A
23. D
24. B
25. A

TEST 2

DIRECTIONS: Each question or incomplete statement is followed by several suggested answers or completions. Select the one that BEST answers the question or completes the statement. *PRINT THE LETTER OF THE CORRECT ANSWER IN THE SPACE AT THE RIGHT.*

1. You are asked to implement a separate network for the visitors. What would be the MOST cost-effective solution?
   A. Installing a firewall
   B. Creating a VLAN
   C. Installing a VPN
   D. None of the above

2. A user complains that he is not able to send an email to his fellow user at the company and you believe that it is a DNS-related issue. After typing *nslookup*, the _____ command will allow finding out the IP address of the company's mail server.
   A. set type=ptr
   B. set type=mx
   C. set type=soa
   D. none of the above

3. The _____ command will allow you to find out the DNS servers configured on a computer.
   A. nslookup
   B. nbtstat
   C. netstat
   D. none of the above

4. A multiple devices network has to be set with a smaller broadcast domain while remaining on a small budget. The best solution is to
   A. create VLANs
   B. implement more switches
   C. implement more hubs
   D. none of the above

5. If users at your company are not able to connect to servers using the FQDN, the likely cause of this issue would be the _____ is not enabled.
   A. DHCP
   B. DNS
   C. WINS
   D. none of the above

6. If you need to extend the range of the wireless network in your office without running wires throughout the office, which of the following should you implement?
   A. At the end of the office install a repeater
   B. In the middle of the office install a WAP
   C. Both A and B
   D. None of the above

7. You are troubleshooting a network error using a laptop as a network sniffer and are able to see all the communications on the network. What network device is the laptop plugged into?
   A. Router
   B. Gateway
   C. Hub
   D. None of the above

8. To provide the users with better network performance for accessing Internet websites, you should install
   A. traffic shaping
   B. load balancing
   C. caching engine
   D. none of the above

9. After gathering information about a client's network issue and determining the affected area, you will
   A. test the best solution
   B. check for any recent changes in the network
   C. none of the above
   D. both A and B

10. Some users complain that they are not able to access the network. The computers that are not able to access the network carry an IP address of 169.254.0.1. The _____ network service should be checked for troubleshooting.
    A. TFTP
    B. DNS
    C. BOOTP
    D. DHCP

11. You are in charge of several remote servers in the United States. Users call and complain that they are not able to connect to the company's resources that are located on those servers. Which command would you use to verify whether the servers are running?
    A. Ping
    B. Nbstat
    C. Netstat
    D. Telnet

12. A user's star network connected workstation is not able to connect to the network resources. You should first check the
    A. installed network drivers
    B. link lights on the switch
    C. link lights on the network card
    D. none of the above

13. You should be aware of _____ while installing a wireless network in a multiple-floor building.
    A. SSID naming
    B. channel overlap
    C. frequency configuration
    D. none of the above

14. You are contacted by a user. According to him, his system is not able to connect to a file server. After troubleshooting and successfully resolving the issue, you should
    A. create an action plan
    B. document the solution
    C. reboot the server
    D. none of the above

15. A user's computer is affected with an automated application without the user interaction. You should tell the user that this issue is referred to as a
    A. trojan
    B. worm
    C. smurf attack
    D. none of the above

16. You are troubleshooting an application that is frequently terminating. What can be used to determine the problem?
    A. History log
    B. DNS log
    C. Port scanner
    D. Application log

17. A network issue has just been reported to you. Which of the following steps should you take first to troubleshoot the issue?
    A. Ask the user to explain the symptoms in detail
    B. Ask the user about what documentation they had in the past
    C. Record the solution in appropriate logs
    D. None of the above

18. A user complains that after his transfer from the accounting team to HR team he can only print to the accounting team printer and not the HR team printer. What is the cause of this problem?
    A. Wrong DNS
    B. Wrong gateway
    C. Wrong host file
    D. Wrong VLAN

19. If five computers are connected to a single server for file and printing and one computer is not able to connect to the network while the others work properly, this could be caused by
    A. failure of the switch
    B. failure of the server
    C. failure of the NIC
    D. the computer's OS needing to be updated

20. _____ is commonly used to test the fiber connectivity.
    A. Multimeter
    B. Butt set
    C. Toner probe
    D. OTDR

21. A user demands a fault-tolerant server. To provide him with this in a most cost-effective way, you should install
    A. a single router
    B. a single fiber NIC
    C. two NICs for teaming
    D. none of the above

22. A user is having issues accessing the shared resources on the file server. You should first
    A. test the results
    B. identify the symptoms
    C. document the problem
    D. none of the above

23. A user complains that her wireless connection has decreased signal strength, whereas the network configuration has not been changed. The MOST likely cause of the decreased signals is
    A. standards mismatch
    B. incorrect SSID
    C. environmental factors
    D. incorrect encryption

24. A user complains that his wireless 802.11g Internet connection is disrupted. What might be the cause of the problem?
    A. Cell phone
    B. Incandescent light
    C. Cordless phone
    D. Infrared printer

25. You have been asked to retrieve device statistics, errors and information. 25.____
    Which of the following should you use?
    A. SNMP
    B. SMTP
    C. Packet sniffer
    D. TFTP

KEY (CORRECT ANSWERS)

1.	B		11.	A
2.	B		12.	C
3.	A		13.	B
4.	A		14.	B
5.	B		15.	B
6.	B		16.	D
7.	C		17.	A
8.	C		18.	D
9.	B		19.	C
10.	D		20.	D

21. C
22. B
23. C
24. C
25. A

TEST 3

DIRECTIONS: Each question or incomplete statement is followed by several suggested answers or completions. Select the one that BEST answers the question or completes the statement. *PRINT THE LETTER OF THE CORRECT ANSWER IN THE SPACE AT THE RIGHT.*

1. A user is reporting slow network response in his class. The class needs many students to be able to access the same website every day. According to you, which of the following is the BEST remedy for this problem?
   A. Firewall
   B. Caching engine
   C. Fault tolerance
   D. Jitter correction

2. A user complains that he has moved a VoIP phone to a new location. The phone does not start now when it is plugged into the network. The reason for this is that
   A. the phone requires a fiber port
   B. Qos is not enabled on the switch
   C. the switch does not support PoE
   D. none of the above

3. A port scanner is used to
   A. secure switches and routers
   B. find routers with weak passwords
   C. find open ports on network hosts
   D. none of the above

4. A remote web server is not blocked by a firewall. To verify that, a _____ should be used.
   A. port scanner
   B. toner probe
   C. packet injector
   D. none of the above

5. For the purpose of providing redundant paths to network resources, if a link fails, _____ switch features will be needed by you to accomplish the task.
   A. trunking
   B. PoE
   C. VLAN
   D. spanning tree

6. To connect a user to a WPA-encrypted network, you will require a
   A. pre-shared key
   B. PIN
   C. SSID
   D. none of the above

7. Network-based _____ is the most cost-effective technology for protecting a large amount of networked workstations from external attacks.
   A. firewall
   B. IDS
   C. IPS
   D. none of the above

8. After installing and testing a new wireless network for your client and turning wireless access on, you should
   A. document the physical layout
   B. configure wireless adapters
   C. configure the DHCP server
   D. none of the above

9. A ping _____ command would check the loopback adapter of an internal NIC.
   A. 127.1.1.1
   B. 127.0.0.1
   C. 127.127.0.0
   D. none of the above

10. To prevent broadcast storms for your client, you should enable
    A. DHCP
    B. port mirroring
    C. bonding
    D. spanning tree

11. You are configuring a router for SOHO network. You have disabled DHCP service and replaced the IP address scheme on the router. Now you have to establish the connection while keeping the router's current configuration state. What would be the BEST solution?
    A. Assign a static IP address so the PC matches the router
    B. Use APIPA to connect the PC to the router
    C. Both A and B
    D. None of the above

12. When you are configuring a wireless access point, select the channel
    A. frequency range least used in a given area
    B. closest to that configured on neighboring access points
    C. that is the same channel configured on the neighboring access points
    D. none of the above

13. A client has accidentally unplugged the network cable of their computer (in a wired bus topology environment). Which of the following is TRUE?
    A. It will not function until the wires are reconnected
    B. It will function with minimal downtime
    C. It will function with no downtime
    D. None of the above

14. A user complains that he can access the network shares and his email but cannot access any website. Which command tools will you use to begin troubleshooting?
    A. Trace route to any website to determine where the disconnection is happening
    B. Use route add command
    C. Use ping command
    D. None of the above

15. Users at a branch office complain that access to static web content is very slow from their location. Which of the following will improve WAN utilization?
    A. A traffic shaper
    B. An application level firewall
    C. A caching proxy server at the branch
    D. None of the above

16. Your head asks you to verify the available phone numbers at your company. Which of the following should you use to verify the available numbers?
    A. Multimeter
    B. Toner probe
    C. Punch down tool
    D. Butt set

17. You need to run a network for your company, which should be able to handle 30 Mbps data-transfer speeds while keeping the installation cost of the network down. Which cable types would you prefer?
    A. CAT3
    B. CAT6
    C. CAT5e
    D. CAT1

18. You are troubleshooting an issue where a computer is not connecting to the Internet employing a wireless access point. The computer is transferring files locally to the other machines but is unable to reach the Internet. The IP address and default gateways are both on the 182.158.1.0/24. The problem is that the computer
    A. gateway is not routing to a public IP address
    B. is using an invalid IP address
    C. is not using a private IP address
    D. none of the above

19. You have to set up a connection that enables visitors to connect to the Internet but not the server, while employees will be able to connect to both. The same switch manages all of the connections. What should be used to meet these requirements?
    A. OSPF
    B. RIP
    C. Post trunking
    D. VLAN

20. An employee kitchen area is added to your office. No changes have been made in the work area and equipment, but the employees are having a wireless connectivity problem. What is the cause of the problem?
    A. Interference
    B. Distance
    C. Encryption
    D. None of the above

21. If the staff is trained about implementing a set of procedures and policies that makes clear that corporation information is confidential, _____ can be prevented.
    A. social engineering
    B. patch management
    C. smurf attacks
    D. none of the above

22. A user support analyst must be able to manage
    A. his time
    B. his client's time
    C. both A and B
    D. managing time is not necessary in this matter

23. A user support analyst must be able to
    A. consider the relative costs
    B. consider the benefits of potential actions to select the most appropriate one
    C. both A and B
    D. none of the above

24. A user support analyst should
    A. always solve the problems himself
    B. teach users to solve the minor problems themselves
    C. never let users solve the problem
    D. none of the above

25. The user support analyst should have the ability to
    A. communicate information and ideas
    B. read and understand information
    C. identify and understand the speech of another person
    D. all of the above

KEY (CORRECT ANSWERS)

1.	B		11.	A
2.	C		12.	A
3.	C		13.	A
4.	A		14.	A
5.	D		15.	C
6.	A		16.	D
7.	A		17.	C
8.	A		18.	A
9.	B		19.	D
10.	D		20.	A

21. A
22. C
23. C
24. B
25. D

TEST 4

DIRECTIONS: Each question or incomplete statement is followed by several suggested answers or completions. Select the one that BEST answers the question or completes the statement. *PRINT THE LETTER OF THE CORRECT ANSWER IN THE SPACE AT THE RIGHT.*

1. You are troubleshooting the phone service at a site and discover that there is no dial tone present in the connection on block 65. Which tool would you use to check the connection at the demarcation point?
   A. Toner probe   B. Multimeter   C. Cable tester   D. Butt set

2. A client calls you to troubleshoot his machine and you need to open connections and see the current NetBIOS configuration. Which command would you use to display this information?
   A. nbstat   B. msconfig   C. netstat   D. ipconfig

3. A client asks you to implement a new wireless network and run the highest level of wireless encryption. You should run
   A. WEP   B. WPA2 TKIP   C. WPAS AES   D. TTL

4. Which of the following tools is used for capturing username and passwords on a network?
   A. Proxy server   B. Sniffer   C. Firewall   D. Honey pot

5. A company consists of one headquarters and eight remote sites. The remote sites just need to communicate with the headquarters. Which topology is BEST for the company?
   A. Mesh   B. Star   C. Hybrid   D. Ring

6. Which of the following command line tools would you use to verify DNS functionality?
   A. netstat   B. arp   C. dig   D. traceroute

7. Which of the following would you use to provide the highest level of security to a newly installed wireless router?
   A. SSL   B. WEP   C. WPA   D. IPSec

8. An application layer firewall can filter _____, while a network layer firewall cannot.
   A. HTTP URLs
   B. ICMP
   C. Telnet traffic
   D. HTTP traffic

9. What should be used for the purpose of connecting multiple network hosts when the physical signal is being repeated to all ports?
   A. Bridge   B. Hub   C. Router   D. Switch

10. While troubleshooting you need to catch a specific NICs MAC address. While you know the IP address of the NIC, _____ would enable you to discover the MAC address without going to that specific computer physically.
    A. netstat B. ping C. nbstat D. arp

11. A VoIP telephone with a built-in hub is plugged into a single network, using both of the ports (hub port and telephone port). Suddenly, the network starts to experience lag because of the increase in traffic. What would help to avoid this situation in the future?
    A. VLANs
    B. Trunking
    C. Port mirroring
    D. Spanning tree

12. _____ is the MOST secure access method.
    A. RSH B. SNMPv1 C. SFTP D. RCP

13. If you need to access files on a remote server, _____ would be used.
    A. ARP B. FTP C. SIP D. NTP

14. _____ is 568B standard.
    A. Logical network diagram
    B. Network baseline
    C. Wiring schematic
    D. None of the above

15. A user complains that on a wireless network he can connect to local resources but cannot connect to the Internet. Which of the following might be the reason?
    A. The gateway is not configured on the router
    B. The wireless network card is not in range
    C. The wireless network card is not working
    D. None of the above

16. _____ is a client-server based authentication software system that keeps user profiles in a central database.
    A. RADIUS B. MSCHAp C. EAP D. CHAP

17. _____ is an authentication protocol the employs plain text for transmitting passwords over the internet.
    A. Kerberos B. CHAP C. PAP D. RADIUS

18. A user wants to bond his new printer with his PDA. What is the BEST technology to describe the type of wireless printer?
    A. Wi-Fi B. Bluetooth C. IEEE 1394 D. 802.11a

19. Many workstations have lost network connectivity in network. Which of the following steps should you take to troubleshoot the issue?
    A. Document all possible causes
    B. Reboot the computer
    C. Escalate the issue to a senior network associate
    D. None of the above

3 (#4)

20. You need to provide a solution that will allow 500 users of a remote site to access the Internet using only one public routable IP address, allowing direct user access to the Internet. What is the BEST technology to implement?
    A. DNS   B. PAT   C. VPN   D. DHCP

21. You discover that unencrypted passwords are being sent over the network. Which network monitoring utility was used to find this out?
    A. Network scanner
    B. Packet sniffer
    C. Throughput tester
    D. None of the above

22. _____ would need to be installed to connect a fiber NIC with an Ethernet backbone.
    A. Bridge
    B. Hub
    C. Repeater
    D. None of the above

23. _____ is the MOST essential component for providing user support.
    A. Communication
    B. Knowledge
    C. Experience
    D. None of the above

24. To get to the heart of the problem, the support analyst must
    A. listen to the user
    B. not ask questions to the user
    C. ask the right question
    D. both A and C

25. The user should be kept _____ by the support analyst.
    A. informed of progress
    B. informed of expected next steps
    C. both A and B
    D. informed of all technical details

KEY (CORRECT ANSWERS)

1.	D		11.	D
2.	A		12.	C
3.	C		13.	B
4.	B		14.	C
5.	D		15.	A
6.	C		16.	A
7.	C		17.	C
8.	A		18.	B
9.	B		19.	C
10.	D		20.	C

21. B
22. B
23. A
24. D
25. C

PREPARING WRITTEN MATERIAL

PARAGRAPH REARRANGEMENT
COMMENTARY

The sentences that follow are in scrambled order. You are to rearrange them in proper order and indicate the letter choice containing the correct answer at the space at the right.

Each group of sentences in this section is actually a paragraph presented in scrambled order. Each sentence in the group has a place in that paragraph; no sentence is to be left out. You are to read each group of sentences and decide upon the best order in which to put the sentences so as to form a well-organized paragraph.

The questions in this section measure the ability to solve a problem when all the facts relevant to its solution are not given.

More specifically, certain positions of responsibility and authority require the employee to discover connection between events sometimes, apparently, unrelated. In order to do this, the employee will find it necessary to correctly infer that unspecified events have probably occurred or are likely to occur. This ability becomes especially important when action must be taken on incomplete information.

Accordingly, these questions require competitors to choose among several suggested alternatives, each of which presents a different sequential arrangement of the events. Competitors must choose the MOST logical of the suggested sequences.

In order to do so, they may be required to draw on general knowledge to infer missing concepts or events that are essential to sequencing the given events. Competitors should be careful to infer only what is essential to the sequence. The plausibility of the wrong alternatives will always require the inclusion of unlikely events or of additional chains of events which are NOT essential to sequencing the given events.

It's very important to remember that you are looking for the best of the four possible choices, and that the best choice of all may not even be one of the answers you're given to choose from.

There is no one right way to solve these problems. Many people have found it helpful to first write out the order of the sentences, as they would have arranged them, on their scrap paper before looking at the possible answers. If their optimum answer is there, this can save them some time. If it isn't, this method can still give insight into solving the problem. Others find it most helpful to just go through each of the possible choices, contrasting each as they go along. You should use whatever method feels comfortable and works for you.

While most of these types of questions are not that difficult, we've added a higher percentage of the difficult type, just to give you more practice. Usually there are only one or two questions on this section that contain such subtle distinctions that you're unable to answer confidently. And you then may find yourself stuck deciding between two possible choices, neither of which you're sure about.

EXAMINATION SECTION
TEST 1

DIRECTIONS: The following groups of sentences need to be arranged in an order that makes sense. Select the letter preceding the sequence that represents the BEST sentence order. *PRINT THE LETTER OF THE CORRECT ANSWER IN THE SPACE AT THE RIGHT.*

1.   I. The keyboard was purposely designed to be a little awkward to slow typists down.
    II. The arrangement of letters on the keyboard of a typewriter was not designed for the convenience of the typist.
    III. Fortunately, no one is suggesting that a new keyboard be designed right away.
    IV. If one were, we would have to learn to type all over again.
    V. The reason was that the early machines were slower than the typists and would jam easily.
    The CORRECT answer is:
    A. I, III, IV, II, V
    B. II, V, I, IV, III
    C. V, I, II, III, IV
    D. II, I, V, III, IV

2.   I. The majority of the new service jobs are part-time or low-paying.
    II. According to the U.S. Bureau of Labor Statistics, jobs in the service sector constitute 72% of all jobs in this country.
    III. If more and more workers receive less and less money, who will buy the goods and services needed to keep the economy going?
    IV. The service sector is by far the fastest growing part of the United States economy.
    V. Some economists look upon this trend with great concern.
    The CORRECT answer is:
    A. II, IV, I, V, III
    B. II, III, IV, I, V
    C. V, IV, II, III, I
    D. III, I, II, IV, V

3.   I. They can also affect one's endurance.
    II. This can stabilize blood sugar levels, and ensure that the brain is receiving a steady, constant, supply of glucose, so that one is *hitting on all cylinders* while taking the test.
    III. By food, we mean real food, not junk food or unhealthy snacks.
    IV. For this reason, it is important not to skip a meal, and to bring food with you to the exam.
    V. One's blood sugar levels can affect how clearly one is able to think and concentrate during an exam.
    The CORRECT answer is:
    A. V, IV, II, III, I
    B. V, II, I, IV, III
    C. V, I, IV, III, II
    D. V, IV, I, III, II

4. I. Those who are the embodiment of desire are absorbed in material quests, and those who are the embodiment of feeling are warriors who value power more than possession.
    II. These qualities are in everyone, but in different degrees.
    III. But those who value understanding yearn not for goods or victory, but for knowledge.
    IV. According to Plato, human behavior flows from three main sources: desire, emotion, and knowledge.
    V. In the perfect state, the industrial forces would produce but not rule, the military would protect but not rule, and the forces of knowledge, the philosopher kings, would reign.
    The CORRECT answer is:
    A. IV, V, I, II, III
    B. V, I, II, III, IV
    C. IV, III, II, I, V
    D. IV, II, I, III, V

5. I. Of the more than 26,000 tons of garbage produced daily in New York City, 12,000 tons arrive daily at Fresh Kills.
    II. In a month, enough garbage accumulates there to fill the Empire State Building.
    III. In 1937, the Supreme Court halted the practice of dumping the trash of New York City into the sea.
    IV. Although the garbage is compacted, in a few years the mounds of garbage at Fresh Kills will be the highest points south of Maine's Mount Desert Island on the Eastern Seaboard.
    V. Instead, tugboats now pull barges of much of the trash to Staten Island and the largest landfill in the world, Fresh Kills.
    The CORRECT answer is:
    A. III, V, IV, I, II
    B. III, V, II, IV, I
    C. III, V, I, II, IV
    D. III, II, V, IV, I

6. I. Communists rank equality very high, but freedom very low.
    II. Unlike communists, conservatives place a high value on freedom and a very low value on equality.
    III. A recent study demonstrated that one way to classify people's political beliefs is to look at the importance placed on two words: freedom and equality.
    IV. Thus, by demonstrating how members of these groups feel about the two words, the study has proved to be useful for political analysts in several European countries.
    V. According to the study, socialists and liberals rank both freedom and equality very high, while fascists rate both very low.
    The CORRECT answer is:
    A. III, V, I, II, IV
    B. V, IV, III, I, II
    C. III, V, IV, II, I
    D. III, I, II, IV, V

7. I. "Can there be anything more amazing than this?"
    II. If the riddle is successfully answered, his dead brothers will be brought back to life.
    III. "Even though man sees those around him dying every day," says Dharmaraj, "he still believes and acts as if he were immortal."
    IV. "What is the cause of ceaseless wonder?" asks the Lord of the Lake.
    V. In the ancient epic, The Mahabharata, a riddle is asked of one of the Pandava brothers.
    The CORRECT answer is:
    A. V, II, I, IV, III
    B. V, IV, III, I, II
    C. V, II, IV, III, I
    D. V, II, IV, I, III

8. I. On the contrary, the two main theories—the cooperative (neoclassical) theory and the radical (labor theory)—clearly rest on very different assumptions, which have very different ethical overtones.
    II. The distribution of income is the primary factor in determining the relative levels of material well-being that different groups or individuals attain.
    III. Of all issues in economics, the distribution of income is one of the most controversial.
    IV. The neoclassical theory tends to support the existing income distribution (or minor changes), while the labor theory ends to support substantial changes in the way income is distributed.
    V. The intensity of the controversy reflects the fact that different economic theories are not purely neutral, *detached* theories with no ethical or moral implications.
    The CORRECT answer is:
    A. II, I, V, IV, III
    B. III, II, V, I, IV
    C. III, V, II, I, IV
    D. III, V, IV, I, II

9. I. The pool acts as a broker and ensures that the cheapest power gets used first.
    II. Every six seconds, the pool's computer monitors all of the generating stations in the state and decides which to ask for more power and which to cut back.
    III. The buying and selling of electrical power is handled by the New York Power Pool in Guilderland, New York.
    IV. This is to the advantage of both the buying and selling utilities.
    V. The pool began operation in 1970, and consists of the state's eight electric utilities.
    The CORRECT answer is:
    A. V, I, II, III, IV
    B. IV, II, I, III, V
    C. III, V, I, IV, II
    D. V, III, IV, II, I

10.
   I. Modern English is much simpler grammatically than Old English.
   II. Finnish grammar is very complicated; there are some fifteen cases, for example.
   III. Chinese, a very old language, may seem to be the exception, but it is the great number of characters/words that must be mastered that makes it so difficult to learn, not its grammar.
   IV. The newest literary language—that is, written as well as spoken—is Finish, whose literary roots go back only to about the middle of the nineteenth century.
   V. Contrary to popular belief, the longer a language is been in use the simpler its grammar—not the reverse.

   The CORRECT answer is:
   A. IV, I, II, III, V
   B. V, I, IV, II, III
   C. I, II, IV, III, V
   D. IV, II, III, I, V

KEY (CORRECT ANSWERS)

1.	D	6.	A
2.	A	7.	C
3.	C	8.	B
4.	D	9.	C
5.	C	10.	B

TEST 2

DIRECTIONS: This type of question tests your ability to recognize accurate paraphrasing, well-constructed paragraphs, and appropriate style and tone. It is important that the answer you select contains only the facts or concepts given in the original sentences. It is also important that you be aware of incomplete sentences, inappropriate transitions, unsupported opinions, incorrect usage, and illogical sentence order. Paragraphs that do not include all the necessary facts and concepts, that distort them, or that add new ones are not considered correct.

The format for this section may vary. Sometimes, long paragraphs are given, and emphasis is placed on style and organization. Our first five questions are of this type. Other times, the paragraphs are shorter, and there is less emphasis on style and more emphasis on accurate representation of information. Our second group of five questions are of this nature.

For each of Questions 1 through 10, select the paragraph that BEST expresses the ideas contained in the sentences above it. *PRINT THE LETTER OF THE CORRECT ANSWER IN THE SPACE AT THE RIGHT.*

1. I. Listening skills are very important for managers.
    II. Listening skills are not usually emphasized.
    III. Whenever managers are depicted in books, manuals or the media, they are always talking, never listening.
    IV. We'd like you to read the enclosed handout on listening skills and to try to consciously apply them this week.
    V. We guarantee they will improve the quality of your interactions.

    A. Unfortunately, listening skills are not usually emphasized for managers. Managers are always depicted as talking, never listening. We'd like you to read the enclosed handout on listening skills. Please try to apply these principles this week. If you do, we guarantee they will improve the quality of your interactions.
    B. The enclosed handout on listening skills will be important improving the quality of your interactions. We guarantee it. All you have to do is take sometime this week to read and to consciously try to apply the principles. Listening skills are very important for manages, but they are not usually emphasized. Whenever managers are depicted in books, manuals or the media, they are always talking, never listening.
    C. Listening well is one of the most important skills a manager can have, yet it's not usually given much attention. Think about any representation of managers in books, manuals, or in the media that you may have seen. They're always talking, never listening. We'd like you to read the enclosed handout on listening skills and consciously try to apply them the rest of the week. We guarantee you will see a difference in the quality of your interactions.

1._____

D. Effective listening, one very important tool in the effective manager's arsenal, is usually not emphasized enough. The usual depiction of managers in books, manuals or the media is one in which they are always talking, never listening. We'd like you to read the enclosed handout and consciously try to apply the information contained therein throughout the rest of the week. We feel sure that you will see a marked difference in the quality of your interactions.

2. I. Chekhov wrote three dramatic masterpieces which share certain themes and formats: Uncle Vanya, The Cherry Orchard, and The Three Sisters.
    II. They are primarily concerned with the passage of time and how this erodes human aspirations.
    III. The plays are haunted by the ghosts of the wasted life.
    IV. The characters are concerned with life's lesser problems; however, such as the inability to make decisions, loyalty to the wrong cause, and the inability to be clear.
    V. This results in sweet, almost aching, type of a sadness referred to as Chekhovian.

    2._____

    A. Chekhov wrote three dramatic masterpieces: Uncle Vanya, The Cherry Orchard, and The Three Sisters. These masterpieces share certain themes and formats: the passage of time, how time erodes human aspirations, and the ghosts of wasted life. Each masterpiece is characterized by a sweet, almost aching, type of sadness that has become known as Chekhovian. The sweetness of this sadness hinges on the fact that it is not the great tragedies of life which are destroying these characters, but their minor flaws: indecisiveness, misplaced loyalty, unclarity.
    B. The Cherry Orchard, Uncle Vanya, and The Three Sisters are three dramatic masterpieces written by Chekhov that use similar formats to explore a common theme. Each is primarily concerned with the way that passing time wears down human aspirations, and each is haunted by the ghosts of the wasted life. The characters are shown struggling futilely with the lesser problems of life: indecisiveness, loyalty to the wrong cause, and the inability to be clear. These struggles create a mood of sweet, almost aching, sadness that has become known as Chekhovian.
    C. Chekhov's dramatic masterpieces are, along with The Cherry Orchard, Uncle Vanya, and The Three Sisters. These plays share certain thematic and formal similarities. They are concerned most of all with the passage of time and the way in which time erodes human aspirations. Each play is haunted by the specter of the wasted life. Chekhov's characters are caught, however, by life's lesser snares: indecisiveness, loyalty to the wrong cause, and unclarity. The characteristic mood is a sweet, almost aching type of sadness that has come to be known as Chekhovian.
    D. A Chekhovian mood is characterized by sweet, almost aching, sadness. The term comes from three dramatic tragedies by Chekhov which revolve around the sadness of a wasted life. The three masterpieces (Uncle Vanya, The Three Sisters, and The Cherry Orchard) share the same

theme and format. The plays are concerned with how the passage of time erodes human aspirations. They are peopled with characters who are struggling with life's lesser problems. These are people who are indecisive, loyal to the wrong causes, or are unable to make themselves clear.

3.
   I. Movie previews have often helped producers decide which parts of movies they should take out or leave in.
   II. The first 1933 preview of <u>King Kong</u> was very helpful to the producers because many people ran screaming from the theater and would not return when four men first attacked by Kong were eaten by giant spiders.
   III. The 1950 premiere of <u>Sunset Boulevard</u> resulted in the filming of an entirely new beginning, and a delay of six months in the film's release.
   IV. In the original opening scene, William Holden was in a morgue talking with thirty-six other "corpses" about the ways some of them had died.
   V. When he began to tell them of his life with Gloria Swanson, the audience found this hilarious, instead of taking the scene seriously.

3.____

  A. Movie previews have often helped producers decide what parts of movies they should leave in or take out. For example, the first preview of <u>King Kong</u> in 1933 was very helpful. In one scene, four men were first attacked by Kong and then eaten by giant spiders. Many members of the audience ran screaming from the theater and would not return. The premiere of the 1950 film <u>Sunset Boulevard</u> was also very helpful. In the original opening scene, William Holden was in a morgue with thirty-six other "corpses," discussing the ways some of them had died. When he began to tell them of his life with Gloria Swanson, the audience found this hilarious. They were supposed to take the scene seriously. The result was a delay of six months in the release of the film while a new beginning was added.
  B. Movie previews have often helped producers decide whether they should change various parts of a movie. After the 1933 preview of <u>King Kong</u>, a scene in which four men who had been attacked by Kong were eaten by giant spiders was taken out as many people ran screaming from the theater and would not return. The 1950 premiere of <u>Sunset Boulevard</u> also led to some changes. In the original opening scene, William Holden was in a morgue talking with thirty-six other "corpses" about the ways some of them had died. When he began to tell them of his life with Gloria Swanson, the audience found this hilarious, instead of taking the scene seriously.
  C. What do <u>Sunset Boulevard</u> and <u>King Kong</u> have in common? Both show the value of using movie previews to test audience reaction. The first 1933 preview of <u>King Kong</u> showed that a scene showing four men being eaten by giant spiders after having been attacked by Kong was too frightening for many people. They ran screaming from the theater and couldn't be coaxed back. The 1950 premiere of <u>Sunset Boulevard</u> was also a scream, but not the kind the producers intended. The movie opens

with William Holden lying in a morgue discussing the ways they had died with thirty-six other "corpses." When he began to tell them of his life with Gloria Swanson, the audience couldn't take him seriously. Their laughter caused a six-month delay while the beginning was rewritten.

D. Producers very often use movie previews to decide if changes are needed. The premiere of <u>Sunset Boulevard</u> in 1950 led to a new beginning and a six-month delay in film release. At the beginning, William Holden and thirty-six other "corpses" discuss the ways some of them died. Rather than taking this seriously, the audience thought it was hilarious when he began to tell them of his life with Gloria Swanson. The first 1933 preview of <u>King Kong</u> was very helpful for its producers because one scene so terrified the audience that many of them ran screaming from the theater and would not return. In this particular scene, four men who had first been attacked by Kong were eaten by giant spiders.

4.
I. It is common for supervisors to view employees as "things" to be manipulated.
II. This approach does not motivate employees, nor does the carrot-and-stick approach because employees often recognize these behaviors and resent them.
III. Supervisors can change these behaviors by using self-inquiry and persistence.
IV. The best managers genuinely respect those they work with, are supportive and helpful, and are interested in working as a team with those they supervise.
V. They disagree with the Golden Rule that says "he or she who has the gold makes the rules."

4.____

A. Some managers act as if they think the Golden Rule means "he or she who has the gold makes the rules." They show disrespect to employees by seeing them as "things" to be manipulated. Obviously, this approach does not motivate employees any more than the carrot-and-stick approach motivates them. The employees are smart enough to spot these behaviors and resent them. On the other hand, the managers genuinely respect those they work with, are supportive and helpful, and are interested in working as a team. Self-inquiry and persistence can change even the former type of supervisor into the latter.

B. Many supervisors all into the trap of viewing employees as "things" to be manipulated, or try to motivate them by using a carrot-and-stick approach. These methods do not motivate employees, who often recognize the behaviors and resent them. Supervisors can change these behaviors, however, by using self-inquiry and persistence. The best managers are supportive and helpful, and have genuine respect for those with whom they work. They are interested in working as a team with those they supervise. To them, the Golden Rule is not "he or she who has the gold makes the rules."

C. Some supervisors see employees as "things" to be used or manipulated using a carrot-and-stick technique. These methods don't work. Employees often see through them and resent them. A supervisor who wants to change may do so. The techniques of self-inquiry and persistence can be used to turn him or her into the type of supervisor who doesn't think the Golden Rule is "he or she who has the gold makes the rules." They may become like the best managers who treat those with whom they work with respect and give them help and support. These are the manager who know how to build a team.

D. Unfortunately, many supervisors act as if their employees are objects whose movements they can position at will. This mistaken belief has the same result as another popular motivational technique—the carrot-and-stick approach. Both attitudes can lead to the same result—resentment from those employees who recognize the behaviors for what they are. Supervisors who recognize these behaviors can change through the use of persistence and the use of self-inquiry. It's important to remember that the best managers respect their employees. They readily give necessary help and support and are interested in working as a team with those they supervise. To these managers, the Golden Rule is not "he or she who has the gold makes the rules."

5.
I. The first half of the nineteenth century produced a group of pessimistic poets—Byron, De Musset, Heine, Pushkin, and Leopardi.
II. It also produced a group of pessimistic composers—Schubert, Chopin, Schumann, and even the later Beethoven.
III. Above all, in philosophy, there was the profoundly pessimistic philosopher, Schopenhauer.
IV. The Revolution was dead, the Bourbons were restored, the feudal barons were reclaiming their land, and progress everywhere was being suppressed, as the great age was over.
V. "I thank God," said Goethe, "that I am not young in so thoroughly finished a world."

A. "I thank God," said Goethe, "that I am not young in so thoroughly finished a world." The Revolution was dead, the Bourbons were restored, the feudal barons were reclaiming their land, and progress everywhere was being suppressed. The first half of the nineteenth century produced a group of pessimistic poets: Byron, De Musset, Heine, Pushkin, and Leopardi. It also produced pessimistic composers: Schubert, Chopin, Schumann. Although Beethoven came later, he fits into this group, too. Finally and above all, it also produced a profoundly pessimistic philosopher, Schopenhauer. The great age was over.

B. The first half of the nineteenth century produced a group of pessimistic poets: Byron, De Musset, Heine, Pushkin, and Leopardi. It produced a group of pessimistic composers: Schubert, Chopin, Schumann, and even the later Beethoven. Above all, it produced a profoundly pessimistic philosopher, Schopenhauer. For each of these men, the great age was over. The Revolution was dead, and the Bourbons were restored. The feudal barons were reclaiming their land, and progress everywhere was being suppressed.

5._____

C. The great age was over. The Revolution was dead—the Bourbons were restored, and the feudal barons were reclaiming their land. Progress everywhere was being suppressed. Out of this climate came a profound pessimism. Poets, like Byron, De Musset, Heine, Pushkin, and Leopardi; composers, like Schubert, Chopin, Schumann, and even the later Beethoven; and above all, a profoundly pessimistic philosopher, Schopenauer. This pessimism which arose in the first half of the nineteenth century is illustrated by these words of Goethe, "I thank God that I am not young in so thoroughly finished a world."

D. The first half of the nineteenth century produced a group of pessimistic poets, Byron, De Musset, Heine, Pushkin, and Leopardi—and a group of pessimistic composers, Schubert, Chopin, Schumann, and the later Beethoven. Above it all, it produced a profoundly pessimistic philosopher, Schopenhauer. The great age was over. The Revolution was dead, the Bourbons were restored, the feudal barons were reclaiming their land, and progress everywhere was being suppressed. "I thank God," said Goethe, "that I am not young in so thoroughly finished a world."

6.
I. A new manager sometimes may feel insecure about his or her competence in the new position.
II. The new manager may then exhibit defensive or arrogant behavior towards those one supervises, or the new manager may direct overly flattering behavior toward one's new supervisor.

A. Sometimes, a new manager may feel insecure about his or her ability to perform well in this new position. The insecurity may lead him or her to treat others differently. He or she may display arrogant or defensive behavior towards those he or she supervises, or be overly flattering to his or her new supervisor.
B. A new manager may sometimes feel insecure about his or her ability to perform well in the new position. He or she may then become arrogant, defensive, or overly flattering towards those he or she works with.
C. There are times when a new manager may be insecure about how well he or she can perform in the new job. The new manager may also behave defensive or act in an arrogant way towards those he or she supervises, or overly flatter his or her boss.
D. Sometimes a new manager may feel insecure about his or her ability to perform well in the new position. He or she may then display arrogant or defensive behavior towards those they supervise, or become overly flattering towards their supervisors.

7.
I. It is possible to eliminate unwanted behavior by bringing it under stimulus control—tying the behavior to a cue, and then never, or rarely, giving the cue.
II. One trainer successfully used this method to keep an energetic young porpoise from coming out of her tank whenever she felt like it, which was potentially dangerous.
III. Her trainer taught her to do it for a reward, in response to a hand signal, and then rarely gave the signal.

A. Unwanted behavior can be eliminated by tying the behavior to a cue, and then never, or rarely, giving the cue. This is called stimulus control. One trainer was able to use this method to keep an energetic young porpoise from coming out of her tank by teaching her to come out for a reward in response to a hand signal, and then rarely giving the signal.
B. Stimulus control can be used to eliminate unwanted behavior. In this method, behavior is tied to a cue, and then the cue is rarely, if ever, given. One trainer was able to successfully use stimulus control to keep an energetic young porpoise from coming out of her tank whenever she felt like it—a potentially dangerous practice. She taught the porpoise to come out for a reward when she gave a hand signal, and then rarely gave the signal.
C. It is possible to eliminate behavior that is undesirable by bringing it under stimulus control by tying behavior to a signal, and then rarely giving the signal. One trainer successfully used this method to keep an energetic porpoise from coming out of her tank, a potentially dangerous situation. Her trainer taught the porpoise to do it for a reward, in response to a hand signal, and then would rarely give the signal.
D. By using stimulus control, it is possible to eliminate unwanted behavior by tying the behavior to a cue, and then rarely or never give the cue. One trainer was able to use this method to successfully stop a young porpoise from coming out of her tank whenever she felt like it. To curb this potentially dangerous practice, the porpoise was taught by the trainer to come out of the tank for a reward, in response to a hand signal, and then rarely given the signal.

8.
I. There is a great deal of concern over the safety of commercial trucks, caused by their greatly increased role in serious accidents since federal deregulation in 1981.
II. Recently, 60 percent of trucks in New York and Connecticut and 70 percent of trucks in Maryland randomly stopped by state troopers failed safety inspections.
III. Sixteen states in the United States require no training at all for truck drivers.

8._____

A. Since federal deregulation in 1981, there has been a great deal of concern over the safety of commercial trucks, and their greatly increased role in serious accidents. Recently, 60 percent of trucks in New York and Connecticut, and 70 percent of trucks in Maryland failed safety inspections. Sixteen states in the United States require no training at all for truck drivers.
B. There is a great deal of concern over the safety of commercial trucks since federal deregulation in 1981. Their role in serious accidents has greatly increased. Recently, 60 percent of trucks randomly stopped in Connecticut and New York and 70 percent in Maryland failed safety inspections conducted by state troopers. Sixteen states in the United States provide no training at all for truck drivers.
C. Commercial trucks have a greatly increased role in serious accidents since federal deregulation in 1981. This has led to a great deal of concern.

Recently, 70 percent of trucks in Maryland and 60 percent of trucks in New York and Connecticut failed inspection of those that were randomly stopped by state troopers. Sixteen states in the United States require no training for all truck drivers.

D. Since federal deregulation in 1981, the role that commercial trucks have played in serious accidents has greatly increased, and this has led to a great deal of concern. Recently, 60 percent of trucks in New York and Connecticut, and 70 percent of trucks in Maryland randomly stopped by state troopers failed safety inspections. Sixteen states in the U.S. don't require any training for truck drivers.

9.
I. No matter how much some people have, they still feel unsatisfied and want more, or want to keep what they have forever.
II. One recent television documentary showed several people flying from New York to Paris for a one-day shopping spree to buy platinum earrings, because they were bored.
III. In Brazil, some people were ordering coffins that cost a minimum of $45,000 and are equipping them with deluxe stereos, televisions, and other graveyard necessities.

9.____

A. Some people, despite having a great deal, still feel unsatisfied and want more, or think they can keep what they have forever. One recent documentary on television showed several people enroute from Paris to New York for a one day shopping spree to buy platinum earrings, because they were bored. Some people in Brazil are even ordering coffins equipped with such graveyard necessities as deluxe stereos and televisions. The price of the coffins start at $45,000.
B. No matter how much some people have, they may feel unsatisfied. This leads them to want more, or to want to keep what they have forever. Recently, a television documentary depicting several people flying from New York to Paris for a one day shopping spree to buy platinum earrings. They were bored. Some people in Brazil are ordering coffins that cost at least $45,000 and come equipped with deluxe televisions, stereos and other necessary graveyard items.
C. Some people will be dissatisfied no matter how much they have. They may want more, or they may want to keep what they have forever. One recent television documentary showed several people, motivated by boredom, jetting from New York to Paris for a one-day shopping spree to buy platinum earrings. In Brazil, some people are ordering coffins equipped with deluxe stereos, televisions and other graveyard necessities. The minimum price for these coffins—$45,000.
D. Some people are never satisfied. No matter how much they have they still want more, or think they can keep what they have forever. One television documentary recently showed several people flying from New York to Paris for the day to buy platinum earrings because they were bored. In Brazil, some people are ordering coffins that cost $45,000 and are equipped with deluxe stereos, televisions and other graveyard necessities.

10.
    I. A television signal or video signal has three parts.
    II. Its parts are the black-and-white portion, the color portion, and the synchronizing (sync) pulses, which keep the picture stable.
    III. Each video source, whether it's a camera or a video-cassette recorder contains its own generator of these synchronizing pulses to accompany the picture that it's sending in order to keep it steady and straight.
    IV. In order to produce a clean recording, a video-cassette recorder must "lock-up" to the sync pulses that are part of the video it is trying to record, and this effort may be very noticeable if the device does not have gunlock.

10.____

    A. There are three parts to a television or video signal: the black-and-white part, the color part, and the synchronizing (sync) pulses, which keep the picture stable. Whether it's a video-cassette recorder or a camera, each video source contains its own pulse that synchronizes and generates the picture it's sending in order to keep it straight and steady. A video-cassette recorder must "lock up" to the sync pulses that are part of the video it's trying to record. If the device doesn't have gunlock, this effort must be very noticeable.
    B. A video signal or television is comprised of three parts: the black-and-white portion, the color portion, and the sync (synchronizing) pulses, which keep the picture stable. Whether it's a camera or a video-cassette recorder, each video source contains its own generator of these synchronizing pulses. These accompany the picture that it's sending in order to keep it straight and steady. A video-cassette recorder must "lock up" to the sync pulses that are part of the video it is trying to record in order to produce a clean recording. This effort may be very noticeable if the device does not have gunlock.
    C. There are three parts to a television or video signal: the color portion, the black-and-white portion, and the sync (synchronizing pulses). These keep the picture stable. Each video source, whether it's a video-cassette recorder or a camera, generates these synchronizing pulses accompanying the picture it's sending in order to keep it straight and steady. If a clean recording is to be produced, a video-cassette recorder must store the sync pulses that are part of the video it is trying to record. This effort may not be noticeable if the device does not have gunlock.
    D. A television signal or video signal has three parts: the black-and-white portion, the color portion, and the synchronizing (sync) pulses. It's the sync pulses which keep the picture stable, which accompany it and keep it steady and straight. Whether it's a camera or a video-cassette recorder, each video source contains its own generator of these synchronizing pulses. To produce a clean recording, a video-cassette recorder must "lock up" to the sync pulses that are part of the video it is trying to record. If the device does not have gunlock, this effort may be very noticeable.

KEY (CORRECT ANSWERS)

1. C
2. B
3. A
4. B
5. D

6. A
7. B
8. D
9. C
10. D

PREPARING WRITTEN MATERIAL

EXAMINATION SECTION

TEST 1

DIRECTIONS: Each of Questions 1 through 5 consists of a sentence which may or may not be an example of good formal English usage. Examine each sentence, considering grammar, punctuation, spelling, capitalization, and awkwardness. Then choose the correct statement about it from the four options below it. If the English usage in the sentence given is better than any of the changes suggested in options B, C, or D, pick option A. (Do not pick an option that will change the meaning of the sentence.) *PRINT THE LETTER OF THE CORRECT ANSWER IN THE SPACE AT THE RIGHT.*

1. I don't know who could possibly of broken it.
   A. This is an example of good formal English usage.
   B. The word "who" should be replaced by the word "whom."
   C. The word "of" should be replaced by the word "have."
   D. The word "broken" should be replaced by the word "broke."

2. Telephoning is easier than to write.
   A. This is an example of good formal English usage.
   B. The word "telephoning" should be spelled "telephoneing."
   C. The word "than" should be replaced by the word "then."
   D. The words "to write" should be replaced by the word "writing."

3. The two operators who have been assigned to these consoles are on vacation.
   A. This is an example of good formal English usage.
   B. A comma should be placed after the word "operators."
   C. The word "who" should be replaced by the word "whom."
   D. The word "are" should be replaced by the word "is."

4. You were suppose to teach me how to operate a plugboard.
   A. This is an example of good formal English usage.
   B. The word "were" should be replaced by the word "was."
   C. The word "suppose" should be replaced by the word "supposed."
   D. The word "teach" should be replaced by the word "learn."

5. If you had taken my advice; you would have spoken with him.
   A. This is an example of good formal English usage.
   B. The word "advice" should be spelled "advise."
   C. The words "had taken" should be replaced by the word "take."
   D. The semicolon should be changed to a comma.

KEY (CORRECT ANSWERS)

1. C
2. D
3. A
4. C
5. D

TEST 2

DIRECTIONS: Select the correct answer. *PRINT THE LETTER OF THE CORRECT ANSWER IN THE SPACE AT THE RIGHT.*

1. The one of the following sentences which is MOST acceptable from the viewpoint of correct grammatical usage is: 1.____
   A. I do not know which action will have worser results.
   B. He should of known better.
   C. Both the officer on the scene, and his immediate supervisor, is charged with the responsibility.
   D. An officer must have initiative because his supervisor will not always be available to answer questions.

2. The one of the following sentences which is MOST acceptable from the viewpoint of correct grammatical usage is: 2.____
   A. Of all the officers available, the better one for the job will be picked.
   B. Strict orders were given to all the officers, except he.
   C. Study of the law will enable you to perform your duties more efficiently.
   D. It seems to me that you was wrong in failing to search the two men.

3. The one of the following sentences which does NOT contain a misspelled word is: 3.____
   A. The duties you will perform are similar to the duties of a patrolman.
   B. Officers must be constantly alert to sieze the initiative.
   C. Officers in this organization are not entitled to special privileges.
   D. Any changes in procedure will be announced publically.

4. The one of the following sentences which does NOT contain a misspelled word is: 4.____
   A. It will be to your advantage to keep your firearm in good working condition.
   B. There are approximately fourty men on sick leave.
   C. Your first duty will be to pursuade the person to obey the law.
   D. Fires often begin in flameable material kept in lockers.

5. The one of the following sentences which does NOT contain a misspelled word is: 5.____
   A. Offices are not required to perform technical maintainance.
   B. He violated the regulations on two occasions.
   C. Every employee will be held responable for errors.
   D. This was his nineth absence in a year.

KEY (CORRECT ANSWERS)

1. D
2. C
3. C
4. A
5. B

TEST 3

DIRECTIONS: Select the correct answer. *PRINT THE LETTER OF THE CORRECT ANSWER IN THE SPACE AT THE RIGHT.*

1. You are answering a letter that was written on the letterhead of the ABC Company and signed by James H. Wood, Treasurer.
   What is usually considered to be the correct salutation to use in your reply?
   A. Dear ABC Company:
   B. Dear Sirs:
   C. Dear Mr. Wood:
   D. Dear Mr. Treasurer:

   1.____

2. Assume that one of your duties is to handle routine letters of inquiry from the public.
   The one of the following which is usually considered to be MOST desirable in replying to such a letter is a
   A. detailed answer handwritten on the original letter of inquiry
   B. phone call, since you can cover details more easily over the phone than in a letter
   C. short letter giving the specific information requested
   D. long letter discussing all possible aspects of the question raised

   2.____

3. The CHIEF reason for dividing a letter into paragraphs is to
   A. make the message clear to the reader by starting a new paragraph for each new topic
   B. make a short letter occupy as much of the page as possible
   C. keep the reader's attention by providing a pause from time to time
   D. make the letter look neat and businesslike

   3.____

4. Your superior has asked you to send an e-mail from your agency to a government agency in another city. He has written out the message and has indicated the name of the government agency.
   When you dictate the message to your secretary, which of the following items that your superior has NOT mentioned must you be sure to include?
   A. Today's date
   B. The full address of the government agency
   C. A polite opening such as "Dear Sirs"
   D. A final sentence such as "We would appreciate hearing from your agency in reply as soon as is convenient for you"

   4.____

5. The one of the following sentences which is grammatically preferable to the others is:
   A. Our engineers will go over your blueprints so that you may have no problems in construction.
   B. For a long time he had been arguing that we, not he, are to blame for the confusion.
   C. I worked on this automobile for two hours and still cannot find out what is wrong with it.
   D. Accustomed to all kinds of hardships, fatigue seldom bothers veteran policemen.

   5.____

KEY (CORRECT ANSWERS)

1. C
2. C
3. A
4. B
5. A

TEST 4

DIRECTIONS: Select the correct answer. *PRINT THE LETTER OF THE CORRECT ANSWER IN THE SPACE AT THE RIGHT.*

1. Suppose that an applicant for a job as snow laborer presents a letter from a former employer stating: "John Smith has a pleasing manner and never got into an argument with his fellow employees. He was never late or absent." This letter
    A. indicates that with some training Smith will make a good snow gang boss
    B. presents no definite evidence of Smith's ability to do snow work
    C. proves definitely that Smith has never done any snow work before
    D. proves definitely that Smith will do better than average work as a snow laborer

    1._____

2. Suppose you must write a letter to a local organization in your section refusing a request in connection with collection of their refuse.
   You should start the letter by
    A. explaining in detail the consideration you gave the request
    B. praising the organization for its service to the community
    C. quoting the regulation which forbids granting the request
    D. stating your regret that the request cannot be granted

    2._____

3. Suppose a citizen writes in for information as to whether or not he may sweep refuse into the gutter. A Sanitation officer answers as follows:
   Dear Sir:
     No person is permitted to litter, sweep, throw or cast, or direct, suffer or permit any person under his control to litter, sweep, throw or cast any ashes, garbage, paper, dust, or other rubbish or refuse into any public street or place, vacant lot, air shaft, areaway, backyard or court.
                          Very truly yours,
                          John Doe
   This letter is *poorly* written CHIEFLY because
    A. the opening is not indented   B. the thought is not clear
    C. the tone is too formal and cold D. there are too many commas used

    3._____

4. A section of a disciplinary report written by a Sanitation officer states: "It is requested that subject Sanitation man be advised that his future activities be directed towards reducing his recurrent tardiness else disciplinary action will be initiated which may result in summary discharge."
   This section of the report is *poorly* written MAINLY because
    A. at least one word is misspelled   B. it is not simply expressed
    C. more than one idea is expressed   D. the purpose is not stated

    4._____

5. A section of a disciplinary report written by an officer states: "He comes in late. He takes too much time for lunch. He is lazy. I recommend his services be dispensed with."
   This section of the report is *poorly* written MAINLY because
    A. it ends with a preposition   B. it is not well organized
    C. no supporting facts are stated   D. the sentences are too simple

    5._____

KEY (CORRECT ANSWERS)

1. B
2. D
3. C
4. B
5. C

EXAMINATION SECTION
TEST 1

DIRECTIONS: Each question or incomplete statement is followed by several suggested answers or completions. Select the one that BEST answers the question or completes the statement. *PRINT THE LETTER OF THE CORRECT ANSWER IN THE SPACE AT THE RIGHT.*

1. Which of the following sentences is punctuated INCORRECTLY?   1.____
   A. Johnson said, "One tiny virus, Blanche, can multiply so fast that it will become 200 viruses in 25 minutes."
   B. With economic pressures hitting them from all sides, American farmers have become the weak link in the food chain.
   C. The degree to which this is true, of course, depends on the personalities of the people involved, the subject matter, and the atmosphere in general.
   D. "What loneliness, asked George Eliot, is more lonely than distrust?"

2. Which of the following sentences is punctuated INCORRECTLY?   2.____
   A. Based on past experiences, do you expect the plumber to show up late, not have the right parts, and overcharge you.
   B. When polled, however, the participants were most concerned that it be convenient.
   C. No one mentioned the flavor of the coffee, and no one seemed to care that china was used instead of plastic.
   D. As we said before, sometimes people view others as things; they don't see them as living, breathing beings like themselves.

3. Convention members travelled here from Kingston New York Pittsfield Massachusetts Bennington Vermont and Hartford Connecticut.   3.____
   How many commas should there be in the above sentence?
   A. 3   B. 4   C. 5   D. 6

4. Of the two speakers the one who spoke about human rights is more famous and more humble.   4.____
   How many commas should there be in the above sentence?
   A. 1   B. 2   C. 3   D. 4

5. Which sentence is punctuated INCORRECTLY?   5.____
   A. Five people voted no; two voted yes; one person abstained.
   B. Well, consider what has been said here today, but we won't make any promises.
   C. Anthropologists divide history into three major periods: the Stone Age, the Bronze Age, and the Iron Age.
   D. Therefore, we may create a stereotype about people who are unsuccessful; we may see them as lazy, unintelligent, or afraid of success.

141

6. Which sentence is punctuated INCORRECTLY?
   A. Studies have found that the unpredictability of customer behavior can lead to a great deal of stress, particularly if the behavior is unpleasant or if the employee has little control over it.
   B. If this degree of emotion and variation can occur in spectator sports, imagine the role that perceptions can play when there are real stakes involved.
   C. At other times, however hidden expectations may sabotage or severely damage an encounter without anyone knowing what happened.
   D. There are usually four issues to look for in a conflict: differences in values, goals, methods, and facts.

Questions 7-10.

DIRECTIONS: Questions 7 through 10 test your ability to distinguish between words that sound alike but are spelled differently and have different meanings. In the following groups of sentences, one of the underlined words is used incorrectly.

7. A. By accepting responsibility for their actions, managers promote trust.
   B. Dropping hints or making illusions to things that you would like changed sometimes leads to resentment.
   C. The entire unit loses respect for the manager and resents the reprimand.
   D. Many people are averse to confronting problems directly; they would rather avoid them.

8. A. What does this say about the effect our expectations have on those we supervise?
   B. In an effort to save time between 9 A.M. and 1 P.M., the staff members devised their own interpretation of what was to be done on these forms.
   C. The taskmaster's principal concern is for getting the work done; he or she is not concerned about the need or interests of employees.
   D. The advisor's main objective was increasing Angela's ability to invest her capitol wisely.

9. A. A typical problem is that people have to cope with the internal censer of their feelings.
   B. Sometimes, in their attempt to sound more learned, people speak in ways that are barely comprehensible.
   C. The council will meet next Friday to decide whether Abrams should continue as representative.
   D. His descent from grace was assured by that final word.

10. A. The doctor said that John's leg had to remain stationary or it would not heal properly.
    B. There is a city ordinance against parking too close to fire hydrants.
    C. Meyer's problem is that he is never discrete when talking about office politics.
    D. Mrs. Thatcher probably worked harder than any other British Prime Minister had ever worked.

Questions 11-20.

DIRECTIONS: For each of the following groups of sentences in Questions 11 through 20, select the sentence which is the BEST example of English usage and grammar.

11. A. She is a woman who, at age sixty, is distinctly attractive and cares about how they look.
    B. It was a seemingly impossible search, and no one knew the problems better than she.
    C. On the surface, they are all sweetness and light, but his morbid character is under it.
    D. The minicopier, designed to appeal to those who do business on the run like architects in the field or business travelers, weigh about four pounds.

11._____

12. A. Neither the administrators nor the union representative regret the decision to settle the disagreement.
    B. The plans which are made earlier this year were no longer being considered.
    C. I would have rode with him if I had known he was leaving at five.
    D. I don't know who she said had it.

12._____

13. A. Writing at a desk, the memo was handed to her for immediate attention.
    B. Carla didn't water Carl's plants this week, which she never does.
    C. Not only are they good workers, with excellent writing and speaking skills, and they get to the crux of any problem we hand them.
    D. We've noticed that this enthusiasm for undertaking new projects sometimes interferes with his attention to detail.

13._____

14. A. It's obvious that Nick offends people by being unruly, inattentive, and having no patience.
    B. Marcia told Genie that she would have to leave soon.
    C. Here are the papers you need to complete your investigation.
    D. Julio was startled by you're comment.

14._____

15. A. The new manager has done good since receiving her promotion, but her secretary has helped her a great deal.
    B. One of the personnel managers approached John and tells him that the client arrived unexpectedly.
    C. If somebody can supply us with the correct figures, they should do so immediately.
    D. Like zealots, advocates seek power because they want to influence the policies and actions of an organization.

15._____

16. A. Between you and me, Chris probably won't finish this assignment in time.
    B. Rounding the corner, the snack bar appeared before us.
    C. Parker's radical reputation made to the Supreme Court his appointment impossible.
    D. By the time we arrived, Marion finishes briefing James and returns to Hank's office.

17. A. As we pointed out earlier, the critical determinant of the success of middle managers is their ability to communicate well with others.
    B. The lecturer stated there wasn't no reason for bad supervision.
    C. We are well aware whose at fault in this instance.
    D. When planning important changes, it's often wise to seek the participation of others because employees often have much valuable ideas to offer.

18. A. Joan had ought to throw out those old things that were damaged when the roof leaked.
    B. I spose he'll let us know what he's decided when he finally comes to a decision.
    C. Carmen was walking to work when she suddenly realized that she had left her lunch on the table as she passed the market.
    D. Are these enough plants for your new office?

19. A. First move the lever forward, and then they should lift the ribbon casing before trying to take it out.
    B. Michael finished quickest than any other person in the office.
    C. There is a special meeting for we committee members today at 4 p.m.
    D. My husband is worried about our having to work overtime next week.

20. A. Another source of conflicts are individuals who possess very poor interpersonal skills.
    B. It is difficult for us to work with him on projects because these kinds of people are not interested in team building.
    C. Each of the departments was represented at the meeting.
    D. Poor boy, he never should of past that truck on the right.

Questions 21-28.

DIRECTIONS: In Questions 21 through 28, there may be a problem with English grammar or usage. If a problem does exist, select the letter that indicates the most effective change. If no problem exists, select Choice A.

21. He rushed her to the hospital and stayed with her, even though this took quite a bit of his time, he didn't charge her anything.
    A. No changes are necessary.
    B. Change even though to although
    C. Change the first comma to a period and capitalize even
    D. Change rushed to had rushed

22. Waiting that appears unfairly feels longer than waiting that seems justified. 22.____
    A. No changes are necessary.
    B. Change unfairly to unfair
    C. Change appears to seems
    D. Change longer to longest

23. May be you and the person who argued with you will be able to reach an agreement. 23.____
    A. No changes are necessary
    B. Change will be to were
    C. Change argued with to had an argument with
    D. Change May be to Maybe

24. Any one of them could of taken the file while you were having coffee. 24.____
    A. No changes are necessary
    B. Change any one to anyone
    C. Change of to have
    D. Change were having to were out having

25. While people get jobs or move from poverty level to better paying employment, they stop receiving benefits and start paying taxes. 25.____
    A. No changes are necessary
    B. Change While to As
    C. Change stop to will stop
    D. Change get to obtain

26. Maribeth's phone rang while talking to George about the possibility of their meeting Tom at three this afternoon. 26.____
    A. No changes are necessary
    B. Change their to her
    C. Move to George so that it follows Tom
    D. Change talking to she was talking

27. According to their father, Lisa is smarter than Chris, but Emily is the smartest of the three sisters. 27.____
    A. No changes are necessary
    B. Change their to her
    C. Change is to was
    D. Make two sentences, changing the second comma to a period and omitting but

28. Yesterday, Mark and he claim that Carl took Carol's ideas and used them inappropriately. 28.____
    A. No changes are necessary
    B. Change claim to claimed
    C. Change inappropriately to inappropriate
    D. Change Carol's to Carols'

Questions 29-34.

DIRECTIONS: For each group of sentences in Questions 29 through 34, select the choice that represents the BEST editing of the problem sentence.

29. The managers expected employees to be at their desks at all times, but they would always be late or leave unannounced.
    A. The managers wanted employees to always be at their desks, but they would always be late or leave unannounced.
    B. Although the managers expected employees to be at their desks no matter what came up, they would always be late and leave without telling anyone.
    C. Although the managers expected employees to be at their desks at all times, the managers would always be late or leave without telling anyone.
    D. The managers expected the employee to never leave their desks, but they would always be late or leave without telling anyone.

29.____

30. The one who is department manager he will call you to discuss the problem tomorrow morning at 10 A.M.
    A. The one who is department manager will call you tomorrow morning at ten to discuss the problem.
    B. The department manager will call you to discuss the problem tomorrow at 10 A.M.
    C. Tomorrow morning at 10 A.M., the department manager will call you to discuss the problem.
    D. Tomorrow morning the department manager will call you to discuss the problem.

30.____

31. A conference on child care in the workplace the $200 cost of which to attend may be prohibitive to childcare workers who earn less than that weekly.
    A. A conference on child care in the workplace that costs $200 may be too expensive for childcare workers who earn less than that each week.
    B. A conference on child care in the workplace, the cost of which to attend is $200, may be prohibitive to childcare workers who earn less than that weekly.
    C. A conference on child care in the workplace who costs $200 may be too expensive for childcare workers who earn less than that a week.
    D. A conference on child care in the workplace which costs $200 may be too expensive to childcare workers who earn less than that on a weekly basis.

31.____

32. In accordance with estimates recently made, there are 40,000 to 50,000 nuclear weapons in our world today.
    A. Because of estimates recently, there are 40,000 to 50,000 nuclear weapons in the world today.
    B. In accordance with estimates made recently, there are 40,000 to 50,000 nuclear weapons in the world today.

32.____

C. According to estimates made recently, there are 40,000 to 50,000 weapons in the world today.
D. According to recent estimates, there are 40,000 to 50,000 nuclear weapons in the world today.

33. Motivation is important in problem solving, but they say that excessive motivation can inhibit the creative process. 33.____
    A. Motivation is important in problem solving, but, as they say, too much of it can inhibit the creative process.
    B. Motivation is important in problem solving and excessive motivation will inhibit the creative process.
    C. Motivation is important in problem solving, but excessive motivation can inhibit the creative process.
    D. Motivation is important in problem solving because excessive motivation can inhibit the creative process.

34. In selecting the best option calls for consulting with all the people that are involved in it. 34.____
    A. In selecting the best option consulting with all people concerned with it.
    B. Calling for the best option, we consulted all the affected people.
    C. We called all the people involved to select the best option.
    D. To be sure of selecting the best option, one should consult all the people involved.

35. There are a number of problems with the following letter. From the options below, select the version that is MOST in accordance with standard business style, tone, and form. 35.____

    Dear Sir:

    We are so sorry that we have had to backorder your order for 15,000 widgets and 2,300 whatzits for such a long time. We have been having incredibly bad luck lately. When your order first came in no one could get to it because my secretary was out with the flu and her replacement didn't know what she was doing, then there was the dock strike in Cucamonga which held things up for awhile, and then it just somehow got lost. We think it may have fallen behind the radiator.
    We are happy to say that all these problems have been taken care of, we are caught up on supplies, and we should have the stuff to you soon, in the near future—about two weeks. You may not believe us after everything you've been through with us, but it's true.
    We'll let you know as soon as we have a secure date for delivery. Thank you so much for continuing to do business with us after all the problems this probably has caused you.

    Yours very sincerely,
    Rob Barker

A. Dear Sir:

　　We are so sorry that we have had to backorder your order for 15,000 widgets and 2,300 whatzits. We have been having problems with staff lately and the dock strike hasn't helped anything.
　　We are happy to say that all these problems have been taken care of. I've told my secretary to get right on it, and we should have the stuff to you soon. Thank you so much for continuing to do business with us after all the problems this must have caused you.
　　We'll let you know as soon as we have a secure date for delivery.

　　Sincerely,
　　Rob Barker

B. Dear Sir:

　　We regret that we haven't been able to fill your order for 15,000 widgets and 2,300 whatzits in a timely fashion.
　　We'll let you know as soon as we have a secure date for delivery.

　　Sincerely,
　　Rob Barker

C. Dear Sir:

　　We are so very sorry that we haven't been able to fill your order for 15,000 widgets and 2,300 whatzits. We have been having incredibly bad luck lately, but things are much better now.
　　Thank you so much for bearing with us through all of this. We'll let you know as soon as we have a secure date for delivery.

　　Sincerely,
　　Rob Barker

D. Dear Sir:

　　We are very sorry that we haven't been able to fill your order for 15,000 widgets and 2,300 whatzits. Due to unforeseen difficulties, we have had to back-order your request. At this time, supplies have caught up to demand, and we foresee a delivery date within the next two weeks.
　　We'll let you know as soon as we have a secure date for delivery. Thank you for your patience.

　　Sincerely,
　　Rob Barker

KEY (CORRECT ANSWERS)

1.	D	11.	B	21.	C	31.	A
2.	A	12.	D	22.	B	32.	D
3.	B	13.	D	23.	D	33.	C
4.	A	14.	C	24.	C	34.	D
5.	B	15.	D	25.	B	35.	D
6.	C	16.	A	26.	D		
7.	B	17.	A	27.	A		
8.	D	18.	D	28.	B		
9.	A	19.	D	29.	C		
10.	C	20.	C	30.	B		

EXAMINATION SECTION
TEST 1

DIRECTIONS: In each of the following questions, only one of the four sentences conforms to standards of correct usage. The other three contain errors in grammar, diction, or punctuation. Select the choice in each question which BEST conforms to standards of correct usage. Consider a choice correct if it contains none of the errors mentioned above, even though there may be other ways of expressing the same thought. *PRINT THE LETTER OF THE CORRECT ANSWER IN THE SPACE AT THE RIGHT.*

1. A. Because he was ill was no excuse for his behavior
    B. I insist that he see a lawyer before he goes to trial.
    C. He said "that he had not intended to go."
    D. He wasn't out of the office only three days.

    1._____

2. A. He came to the station and pays a porter to carry his bags into the train.
    B. I should have liked to live in medieval times.
    C. My father was born in Linville. A little country town where everybody knows everyone else.
    D. The car, which is parked across the street, is disabled.

    2._____

3. A. He asked the desk clerk for a clean, quiet, room.
    B. I expected James to be lonesome and that he would want to go home.
    C. I have stopped worrying because I have heard nothing further on the subject.
    D. If the board of directors controls the company, they may take actions which are disapproved by the stockholders.

    3._____

4. A. Each of the players knew their place.
    B. He whom you saw on the stage is the son of an actor.
    C. Susan is the smartest of the twin sisters.
    D. Who ever thought of him winning both prizes?

    4._____

5. A. An outstanding trait of early man was their reliance on omens.
    B. Because I had never been there before.
    C. Neither Mr. Jones nor Mr. Smith has completed his work.
    D. While eating my dinner, a dog came to the window.

    5._____

6. A. A copy of the lease, in addition to the Rules and Regulations, are to be given to each tenant.
    B. The Rules and Regulations and a copy of the lease is being given to each tenant.
    C. A copy of the lease, in addition to the Rules and Regulations, is to be given to each tenant.
    D. A copy of the lease, in addition to the Rules and Regulations, are being given to each tenant.

    6._____

7. A. Although we understood that for him music was a passion, we were disturbed by the fact that he was addicted to sing along with the soloists.
    B. Do you believe that Steven is liable to win a scholarship?
    C. Give the picture to whomever is a connoisseur of art.
    D. Whom do you believe to be the most efficient worker in the office?

8. A. Each adult who is sure they know all the answers will some day realize their mistake.
    B. Even the most hardhearted villain would have to feel bad about so horrible a tragedy.
    C. Neither being licensed teachers, both aspirants had to pass rigorous tests before being appointed.
    D. The principal reason why he wanted to be designated was because he had never before been to a convention.

9. A. Being that the weather was so inclement, the party has been postponed for at least a month.
    B. He is in New York City only three weeks and he has already seen all the thrilling sights in Manhattan and in the other four boroughs.
    C. If you will look it up in the official directory, which can be consulted in the library during specified hours, you will discover that the chairman and director are Mr. T. Henry Long.
    D. Working hard at college during the day and at the post office during the night, he appeared to his family to be indefatigable.

10. A. I would have been happy to oblige you if you only asked me to do it.
    B. The cold weather, as well as the unceasing wind and rain, have made us decide to spend the winter in Florida.
    C. The politician would have been more successful in winning office if he would have been less dogmatic.
    D. These trousers are expensive; however, they will wear well.

11. A. All except him wore formal attire at the reception for the ambassador.
    B. If that chair were to be blown off of the balcony, it might injure someone below.
    C. Not a passenger, who was in the crash, survived the impact.
    D. To borrow money off friends is the best way to lose them.

12. A. Approaching Manhattan on the ferry boat from Staten Island, an unforgettable sight of the skyscrapers is seen.
    B. Did you see the exhibit of modernistic paintings as yet?
    C. Gesticulating wildly and ranting in stentorian tones, the speaker was the sinecure of all eyes.
    D. The airplane with crew and passengers was lost somewhere in the Pacific Ocean.

13.
  A. If one has consistently had that kind of training, it is certainly too late to change your entire method of swimming long distances.
  B. The captain would have been more impressed if you would have been more conscientious in evacuation drills.
  C. The passengers on the stricken ship were all ready to abandon it at the signal.
  D. The villainous shark lashed at the lifeboat with it's tail, trying to upset the rocking boat in order to partake of it's contents.

14.
  A. As one whose been certified as a professional engineer, I believe that the decision to build a bridge over that harbor is unsound.
  B. Between you and me, this project ought to be completed long before winter arrives.
  C. He fervently hoped that the men would be back at camp and to find them busy at their usual chores.
  D. Much to his surprise, he discovered that the climate of Korea was like his home town.

15.
  A. An industrious executive is aided, not impeded, by having a hobby which gives him a fresh point of view on life and its problems.
  B. Frequent absence during the calendar year will surely mitigate against the chances of promotion.
  C. He was unable to go to the committee meeting because he was very ill.
  D. Mr. Brown expressed his disapproval so emphatically that his associates were embarassed

16.
  A. At our next session, the office manager will have told you something about his duties and responsibilities.
  B. In general, the book is absorbing and original and have no hesitation about recommending it.
  C. The procedures followed by private industry in dealing with lateness and absence are different from ours.
  D. We shall treat confidentially any information about Mr. Doe, to whom we understand you have sent reports to for many years.

17.
  A. I talked to one official, whom I knew was fully impartial.
  B. Everyone signed the petition but him.
  C. He proved not only to be a good student but also a good athlete.
  D. All are incorrect.

18.
  A. Every year a large amount of tenants are admitted to housing projects.
  B. Henry Ford owned around a billion dollars in industrial equipment.
  C. He was aggravated by the child's poor behavior.
  D. All are incorrect.

13.____

14.____

15.____

16.____

17.____

18.____

19. A. Before he was committed to the asylum he suffered from the illusion that he was Napoleon.
     B. Besides stocks, there were also bonds in the safe.
     C. We bet the other team easily.
     D. All are incorrect.

20. A. Bring this report to your supervisory.
     B. He set the chair down near the table.
     C. The capitol of New York is Albany.
     D. All are incorrect.

21. A. He was chosen to arbitrate the dispute because everyone knew he would be disinterested.
     B. It is advisable to obtain the best council before making an important decision.
     C. Less college students are interested in teaching than ever before.
     D. All are incorrect.

22. A. She, hearing a signal, the source lamp flashed.
     B. While hearing a signal, the source lamp flashed.
     C. In hearing a signal, the source lamp flashed.
     D. As she heard a signal, the source lamp flashed.

23. A. Every one of the time records have been initialed in the designated spaces.
     B. All of the time records has been initialed in the designated spaces.
     C. Each one of the time records was initialed in the designated spaces.
     D. The time records all been initialed in the designated spaces.

24. A. If there is no one else to answer the phone, you will have to answer it.
     B. You will have to answer it yourself if no one else answers the phone.
     C. If no one else is not around to pick up the phone, you will have to do it.
     D. You will have to answer the phone when nobodys here to do it.

25. A. Dr. Barnes not in his office. What could I do for you?
     B. Dr. Barnes is not in his office. Is there something I can do for you?
     C. Since Dr. Barnes is not in his office, might there be something I may do for you?
     D. Is there any ways I can assist you since Dr. Barnes is not in his office?

26. A. She do not understand how the new console works.
     B. The way the new console works, she doesn't understand.
     C. She doesn't understand how the new console works.
     D. The new console works, so that she doesn't understand.

27. A. Certain changes in my family income must be reported as they occur.
     B. When certain changes in family income occur, it must be reported.
     C. Certain family income change must be reported as they occur.
     D. Certain changes in family income must be reported as they have been occurring.

28. A. Each tenant has to complete the application themselves.
    B. Each of the tenants have to complete the application by himself.
    C. Each of the tenants has to complete the application himself.
    D. Each of the tenants has to complete the application by themselves.

29. A. Yours is the only building that the construction will effect.
    B. Your's is the only building affected by the construction.
    C. The construction will only effect your building.
    D. Yours is the only building that will be affected by the construction.

30. A. There is four tests left.
    B. The number of tests left are four.
    C. There are four tests left.
    D. Four of the tests remains.

31. A. Each of the applicants takes a test.
    B. Each of the applicant take a test.
    C. Each of the applicants take tests.
    D. Each of the applicants have taken tests.

32. A. The applicant, not the examiners, are ready.
    B. The applicants, not the examiners, is ready.
    C. The applicants, not the examiner, are ready.
    D. The applicant, not the examiner, are ready

33. A. You will not progress except you practice.
    B. You will not progress without you practicing.
    C. You will not progress unless you practice.
    D. You will not progress provided you do not practice.

34. A. Neither the director or the employees will be at the office tomorrow.
    B. Neither the director nor the employees will be at the office tomorrow.
    C. Neither the director, or the secretary nor the other employees will be at the office tomorrow.
    D. Neither the director, the secretary or the other employees will be at the office tomorrow.

35. A. In my absence, he and her will have to finish the assignment.
    B. In my absence he and she will have to finish the assignment.
    C. In my absence she and him, they will have to finish the assignment.
    D. In my absence he and her both will have to finish the assignment.

KEY (CORRECT ANSWERS)

1.	B	11.	A	21.	A	31.	A
2.	B	12.	D	22.	D	32.	C
3.	C	13.	C	23.	C	33.	C
4.	B	14.	B	24.	A	34.	B
5.	C	15.	A	25.	B	35.	B
6.	C	16.	C	26.	C		
7.	D	17.	B	27.	A		
8.	B	18.	D	28.	C		
9.	D	19.	B	29.	D		
10.	D	20.	B	30.	C		

TEST 2

DIRECTIONS: Each question or incomplete statement is followed by several suggested answers or completions. Select the one that BEST answers the question or completes the statement. *PRINT THE LETTER OF THE CORRECT ANSWER IN THE SPACE AT THE RIGHT.*

Questions 1-4.

DIRECTIONS: Questions 1 through 4 consist of three sentences each. For each question, select the sentence which contains NO error in grammar or usage.

1. A. Be sure that everybody brings his notes to the conference.
   B. He looked like he meant to hit the boy.
   C. Mr. Jones is one of the clients who was chosen to represent the district.
   D. All are incorrect.

2. A. He is taller than I.
   B. I'll have nothing to do with these kind of people.
   C. The reason why he will not buy the house is because it is too expensive.
   D. All are incorrect.

3. A. Aren't I eligible for this apartment.
   B. Have you seen him anywheres?
   C. He should of come earlier.
   D. All are incorrect.

4. A. He graduated college in 2022.
   B. He hadn't but one more line to write.
   C. Who do you think is the author of this report?
   D. All are incorrect.

Questions 5-35.

DIRECTIONS: In each of the following questions, only one of the four sentences conforms to standards of correct usage. The other three contain errors in grammar, diction, or punctuation. Select the choice in each question which BEST conforms to standards of correct usage. Consider a choice correct if it contains none of the errors mentioned above, even though there may be other ways of expressing the same thought.

5. A. It is obvious that no one wants to be a kill-joy if they can help it.
   B. It is not always possible, and perhaps it never ispossible, to judge a person's character by just looking at him.
   C. When Yogi Berra of the New York Yankees hit an immortal grandslam home run, everybody in the huge stadium including Pittsburgh fans, rose to his feet.
   D. Every one of us students must pay tuition today.

6. A. The physician told the young mother that if the baby is not able to digest its milk, it should be boiled.
   B. There is no doubt whatsoever that he felt deeply hurt because John Smith had betrayed the trust.
   C. Having partaken of a most delicious repast prepared by Tessie Breen, the hostess, the horses were driven home immediately thereafter.
   D. The attorney asked my wife and myself several questions.

7. A. Despite all denials, there is no doubt in my mind that
   B. At this time everyone must deprecate the demogogic attack made by one of our Senators on one of our most revered statesmen.
   C. In the first game of a crucial two-game series, Ted Williams, got two singles, both of them driving in a run.
   D. Our visitor brought good news to John and I.

8. A. If he would have told me, I should have been glad to help him in his dire financial emergency.
   B. Newspaper men have often asserted that diplomats or so-called official spokesmen sometimes employ equivocation in attempts to deceive.
   C. I think someones coming to collect money for the Red Cross.
   D. In a masterly summation, the young attorney expressed his belief that the facts clearly militate against this opinion.

9. A. We have seen most all the exhibits.
   B. Without in the least underestimating your advice, in my opinion the situation has grown immeasurably worse in the past few days.
   C. I wrote to the box office treasurer of the hit show that a pair of orchestra seats would be preferable.
   D. As the grim story of Pearl Harbor was broadcast on that fateful December 7, it was the general opinion that war was inevitable.

10. A. Without a moment's hesitation, Casey Stengel said that Larry Berra works harder than any player on the team.
    B. There is ample evidence to indicate that many animals can run faster than any human being.
    C. No one saw the accident but I.
    D. Example of courage is the heroic defense put up by the paratroopers against overwhelming odds.

11. A. If you prefer these kind, Mrs. Grey, we shall be more than willing to let you have them reasonably.
    B. If you like these here, Mrs. Grey, we shall be more than willing to let you have them reasonably.
    C. If you like these, Mrs. Grey, we shall be more than willing to let you have them.
    D. Who shall we appoint?

3 (#2)

12. A. The number of errors are greater in speech than in writing.
    B. The doctor rather than the nurse was to blame for his being neglected.
    C. Because the demand for these books have been so great, we reduced the price.
    D. John Galsworthy, the English novelist, could not have survived a serious illness; had it not been for loving care.

12.____

13. A. Our activities this year have seldom ever been as interesting as they have been this month.
    B. Our activities this month have been more interesting, or at least as interesting as those of any month this year.
    C. Our activities this month has been more interesting than those of any other month this year.
    D. Neither Jean nor her sister was at home.

13.____

14. A. George B. Shaw's view of common morality, as well as his wit sparkling with a dash of perverse humor here and there, have led critics to term him "The Incurable Rebel."
    B. The President's program was not always received with the wholehearted endorsement of his own party, which is why the party faces difficulty in drawing up a platform for the coming election.
    C. The reason why they wanted to travel was because they had never been away from home.
    D. Facing a barrage of cameras, the visiting celebrity found it extremely difficult to express his opinions clearly.

14.____

15. A. When we calmed down, we all agreed that our anger had been kind of unnecessary and had not helped the situation.
    B. Without him going into all the details, he made us realize the horror of the accident.
    C. Like one girl, for example, who applied for two positions.
    D. Do not think that you have to be so talented as he is in order to play in the school orchestra.

15.____

16. A. He looked very peculiarly to me.
    B. He certainly looked at me peculiar.
    C. Due to the train's being late, we had to wait an hour.
    D. The reason for the poor attendance is that it is raining.

16.____

17. A. About one out of four own an automobile.
    B. The collapse of the old Mitchell Bridge was caused by defective construction in the central pier.
    C. Brooks Atkinson was well acquainted with the best literature, thus helping him to become an able critic.
    D. He has to stand still until the relief man comes up, thus giving him no chance to move about and keep warm.

17.____

18. A. He is sensitive to confusion and withdraws from people whom he feels are too noisy.
    B. Do you know whether the data is statistically correct?
    C. Neither the mayor or the aldermen are to blame.
    D. Of those who were graduated from high school, a goodly percentage went to college.

18._____

19. A. Acting on orders, the offices were searched by a designated committee.
    B. The answer probably is nothing.
    C. I thought it to be all right to excuse them from class.
    D. I think that he is as successful a singer, if not more successful, than Mary.

19._____

20. A. $360,000 is really very little to pay for such a wellbuilt house.
    B. The creatures looked like they had come from outer space.
    C. It was her, he knew!
    D. Nobody but me knows what to do.

20._____

21. A. Mrs. Smith looked good in her new suit.
    B. New York may be compared with Chicago.
    C. I will not go to the meeting except you go with me.
    D. I agree with this editorial.

21._____

22. A. My opinions are different from his.
    B. There will be less students in class now.
    C. Helen was real glad to find her watch.
    D. It had been pushed off of her dresser.

22._____

23. A. Almost everyone, who has been to California, returns with glowing reports.
    B. George Washington, John Adams, and Thomas Jefferson, were our first presidents.
    C. Mr. Walters, whom we met at the bank yesterday, is the man, who gave me my first job.
    D. One should study his lessons as carefully as he can.

23._____

24. A. We had such a good time yesterday.
    B. When the bell rang, the boys and girls went in the schoolhouse.
    C. John had the worst headache when he got up this morning.
    D. Today's assignment is somewhat longer than yesterday's.

24._____

25. A. Neither the mayor nor the city clerk are willing to talk.
    B. Neither the mayor nor the city clerk is willing to talk.
    C. Neither the mayor or the city clerk are willing to talk.
    D. Neither the mayor or the city clerk is willing to talk.

25._____

26. A. Being that he is that kind of boy, cooperation cannot be expected.
    B. He interviewed people who he thought had something to say.
    C. Stop whomever enters the building regardless of rank or office held.
    D. Passing through the countryside, the scenery pleased us.

26._____

27.
A. The childrens' shoes were in their closet.
B. The children's shoes were in their closet.
C. The childs' shoes were in their closet.
D. The childs' shoes were in his closet.

28.
A. An agreement was reached between the defendant, the plaintiff, the plaintiff's attorney and the insurance company as to the amount of the settlement.
B. Everybody was asked to give their versions of the accident.
C. The consensus of opinion was that the evidence was inconclusive.
D. The witness stated that if he was rich, he wouldn't have had to loan the money.

29.
A. Before beginning the investigation, all the materials related to the case were carefully assembled.
B. The reason for his inability to keep the appointment is because of his injury in the accident.
C. This here evidence tends to support the claim of the defendant.
D. We interviewed all the witnesses who, according to the driver, were still in town.

30.
A. Each claimant was allowed the full amount of their medical expenses.
B. Either of the three witnesses is available.
C. Every one of the witnesses was asked to tell his story.
D. Neither of the witnesses are right.

31.
A. The commissioner, as well as his deputy and various bureau heads, were present.
B. A new organization of employers and employees have been formed.
C. One or the other of these men have been selected.
D. The number of pages in the book is enough to discourage a reader.

32.
A. Between you and me, I think he is the better man.
B. He was believed to be me.
C. Is it us that you wish to see?
D. The winners are him and her.

33.
A. Beside the statement to the police, the witness spoke to no one.
B. He made no statement other than to the police and I.
C. He made no statement to any one else, aside from the police.
D. The witness spoke to no one but me.

34.
A. The claimant has no one to blame but himself.
B. The boss sent us, he and I, to deliver the packages.
C. The lights come from mine and not his car.
D. There was room on the stairs for him and myself.

35. A. Admission to this clinic is limited to patients' inability to pay for medical care.
    B. Patients who can pay little or nothing for medical care are treated in this clinic.
    C. The patient's ability to pay for medical care is the determining factor in his admission to this clinic.
    D. This clinic is for the patient's that cannot afford to pay or that can pay a little for medical care.

35.____

KEY (CORRECT ANSWERS)

1.	A	11.	C	21.	A	31.	D
2.	A	12.	B	22.	A	32.	A
3.	D	13.	D	23.	D	33.	D
4.	C	14.	D	24.	D	34.	A
5.	D	15.	D	25.	B	35.	B
6.	D	16.	D	26.	B		
7.	B	17.	B	27.	B		
8.	B	18.	D	28.	C		
9.	D	19.	B	29.	D		
10.	B	20.	D	30.	C		

www.ingramcontent.com/pod-product-compliance
Lightning Source LLC
Chambersburg PA
CBHW080322020526
44117CB00035B/2613